TACITUS

ANCIENTS IN ACTION

Also available

Catullus
Amanda Hurley

Cleopatra
Susan Walker and Sally-Ann Ashton

Horace
Philip Hills

Lucretius
John Godwin

Ovid: love songs
Genevieve Liveley

Ovid: myth and metamorphosis
Sarah Annes Brown

Spartacus
Theresa Urbainczyk

ANCIENTS IN ACTION

TACITUS

Rhiannon Ash

BRISTOL CLASSICAL PRESS

First published in 2006 by
Bristol Classical Press
an imprint of
Gerald Duckworth & Co. Ltd.
90-93 Cowcross Street, London EC1M 6BF
Tel: 020 7490 7300
Fax: 020 7490 0080
inquiries@duckworth-publishers.co.uk
www.ducknet.co.uk

A catalogue record for this book is available
from the British Library

ISBN 1 85399 687 4
EAN 9781853996870

Typeset by e-type
Printed and bound in Great Britain by
CPI Bath

Contents

Preface

When John Betts, the original driving force behind 'Ancients in Action', first approached me about the possibility of contributing a volume on Tacitus to the series, he memorably explained to me that it was designed for 'the man on the Clapham omnibus'. If you do happen to be reading this book on a bus, then I will have satisfied the letter, if not the spirit, of the series. Still, writing a clear and accessible book for the non-specialist can be a notoriously difficult thing to do. We have all come across books purporting to be helpful introductions to a topic, which in fact are filled with impenetrable prose and irrelevant detail. My hope is that this study will prove engaging for anyone with broad interests in the ancient world, but that it will particularly interest readers who are reluctant for Tacitus to exist in a vacuum, and who also want to get a sense of an ancient author's continuing significance in the twenty-first century. Many classical authors are surprisingly relevant when it comes to contemporary issues, and indeed at times they can seem alarmingly prescient, perhaps Tacitus above all. If you have heard of Tacitus, but not yet read him, then this book is intended to make you want to do precisely that, perhaps even in the original Latin.

You will see that, in keeping with the format of this series, this is a book uncluttered by footnotes. This allowed me a freedom not often available to modern scholars in the University system writing about the Classical world, but it does mean that it was not possible to acknowledge earlier discussions, or to direct readers to other works on points of detail. I hope that in being let off the leash, I have not strayed too far from the path of common sense and clarity. Readers will at least find directions to more substantial discussions by modern scholars at the end of the book. All translations are my own, except where otherwise stated.

I owe John Betts a particularly big debt of gratitude for asking me to write this book in the first place. His energy and determination, particularly in the world of publishing, has done an enormous amount to keep Classics alive (and lively) during times when prevailing fashions did not always favour the discipline. I would also like to take the opportunity to thank my editor, Deborah Blake, who patiently allowed me additional time to complete the project; my partner Gervase Wood, who cheerfully volunteered to be a guinea-pig and read a draft of the entire book; my former colleague Herwig Maehler, who introduced me to the delightful satire of Heinrich Heine; and my former tutors, Barbara Levick and Chris Pelling, both humane, perceptive and witty scholars and teachers. I was exceptionally lucky to be exposed to Tacitus' historiography under their guidance. Last but by no means least, my students, past and present, at University College London and at Cornell, have all helped to shape my thinking over the years.

Illustrations

1

Tacitus before 'History': The So-called 'Minor Works'

Introduction

A happy vicar I might have been
Two hundred years ago
To preach upon eternal doom
And watch my walnuts grow;

But born, alas, in an evil time,
I missed that pleasant haven,
For the hair has grown on my upper lip
And the clergy are all clean-shaven.

George Orwell, 1935

To produce extraordinary literature, music or poetry, it often helps the process if you have someone to react against or hardships to overcome. Oppressive political or social conditions, if imposed on writers with sufficient talent and determination, can generate just the sort of inspiration and creativity that contentment and safety simply will not foster in the same way. It sounds perverse, and of course, it does not always apply: an individual's creative spirit has to be pretty deeply embedded for it to find expression in arduous circumstances. Yet the personal experience of adversity can turn a potentially good writer into a great one.

The testimony of writers themselves is revealing. So, when George Orwell ('Why I Write', 1946) discusses what makes writers produce books, he identifies four crucial factors: sheer egoism, aesthetic enthusiasm, historical impulse and political purpose. Turning the spotlight on himself, he suggests that he is by nature someone in whom the first three factors would normally have outweighed the fourth, but an initial hatred for imperialism stemming from his job in the Indian Imperial Police in Burma, clearly an unhappy experience, followed by his deepening horror at the emergence of Hitler and the Spanish Civil War, made the crucial difference:

> The Spanish war and other events in 1936-37 turned the scale and thereafter I knew where I stood. Every line of serious work that I have written since 1936 has been written, directly or indirectly, AGAINST totalitarianism and FOR democratic socialism, as I understand it. It seems to me nonsense, in a period like our own, to think that one can avoid writing of such subjects .... And looking back through my work, I see that it is invariably where I lacked a POLITICAL purpose that I wrote lifeless books and was betrayed into purple passages, sentences without meaning, decorative adjectives and humbug generally.

In the essay, Orwell expresses a certain nostalgia for the kind of writer that he might have been in different circumstances, but at the same time he acknowledges how deeply and irreversibly the contemporary political scene has shaped and motivated him. Without that stimulus, he claims that he would have written 'ornate or merely descriptive books'. That is not to say that

1. Tacitus before 'History'

Orwell necessarily enjoyed the painful nature of the creative process thrust upon him by the time and place in which he wrote, but he knew that the alternative was to produce what he saw as lifeless, ephemeral and meaningless books.

Orwell's views about the impulse for writing engage significantly with the literary career of the subject of this study, Tacitus. It is crucial to consider the political and social context in which this Roman author produced his first work, the *Agricola*, if we are to appreciate not just his early writing, but also its subsequent development. Tacitus, a Roman senator, born in *c.* AD 56 in south-eastern Gaul, came into the world when the emperor Nero (AD 54-68) was in power, at a time when the Roman people was feeling full of optimism about the potential of this young ruler, so personable and dynamic in comparison with his eccentric and elderly predecessor, Claudius. Nero's tutor, Seneca the Younger, an extraordinarily versatile writer from Spain, in a work written soon after his young protégé became emperor, makes (biased) comparisons with the divine Apollo, who gives his stamp of approval to the glamorous new ruler, as the Fates spin his destiny:

> 'Don't drop those threads, Fates', Phoebus [Apollo] said, 'but let the one who is similar to me in looks and loveliness, who is no less than me in his singing voice, surpass the temporal boundaries of human life. He will initiate a joyful era for the exhausted and shatter the silence of the laws.'
>
> *Apocolocyntosis* 4

The assimilation of Nero and Apollo recurs in contemporary literature, but, as so often with new leaders, the honeymoon

would not last. As Nero wriggled free from the oppressive
clutches of his tutor, Seneca, and his mother, Agrippina the
Younger, the Roman world was faced with a new kind of
emperor, who became ever more susceptible to (what they saw
as) dubious Greek influences, such as performance on the lyre
and in games, rather than devoting himself to good old-fash-
ioned activities such as warfare and the tedious business of
running the empire. The famous image of Nero fiddling while
Rome burned during the great fire in AD 64 is of course exaggerated, but it finds its roots in the Roman aristocracy's intense
disapproval of the direction in which their once popular
emperor was now taking the principate. And naturally, it was
the elite who shaped the historical record, even if the lower
ranks of society rather enjoyed all that lavish public entertainment. According to the historical tradition, Rome was being
'consumed' by Nero's luxurious new palace, the Golden House,
conveniently built on land in the heart of the city left devastated
by the fire, and meanwhile, to pay for such frivolities, Nero
himself was gripped by a dangerous chimaera, as he went on the
hunt for buried treasure: in AD 66, a man called Caesennius
Bassus 'Punic by origin and of disturbed mind' (Tacitus *Annals*
16.1) had drawn the emperor's attention to the discovery of the
Carthaginian queen Dido's gold, allegedly buried for more than
a millennium, but now conveniently located through a dream,
and there for the taking. The imperial treasury was undoubtedly
under serious pressure at the time, but such flimsy hopes were
no way to address the growing financial crisis.

In the end, the debasing of the principate proved too much,
and one of Nero's governors in Spain, Sulpicius Galba, who
came from an ancient patrician family, decided to co-operate

with Julius Vindex, a governor in Gaul, who was instigating revolt against Nero. When that initial uprising failed, Galba himself organised a rebellion, which (paradoxically) the emperor could have crushed if he had put his mind to it, but instead Nero committed suicide in June 68, driven to despair 'more by rumours and dispatches than by force of arms' (Tacitus *Histories* 1.89). This opened up the way for a sickening descent into a series of civil wars, played out on a global scale, but inevitably impacting on individuals in a very personal way. Tacitus' own circle was not immune. His future father-in-law, Agricola, lost his mother when Otho's marauding soldiers killed her on her estate in Liguria in north-west Italy (*Agricola* 7); and his own family in Gaul must have watched in trepidation as Vitellius' victorious soldiers progressed southwards from Germany, through Gaul, and ultimately down to Rome. Perhaps as a teenager, Tacitus even witnessed Vitellius' dubious victory parade at Lugdunum (Lyons), where the might of his soldiers was displayed for all to see (*Histories* 2.59).

The destructive cycle of violence was eventually brought to an end by the accession of Vespasian (AD 69-79), the first member of a new imperial dynasty, the Flavians (AD 69-96). Yet Tacitus, now 14 years old, must already have developed an acute sense of how fragile and ephemeral apparently robust political systems could be and how costly their disintegration was, even on a temporary basis. Although Tacitus has not left us a convenient, personal document like Orwell's essay 'Why I Write', his surviving works, each in a different way, as we will see, eloquently articulate the fundamental impact of the contemporary scene on his own literary consciousness and reveal for posterity why he wrote.

If the Roman political situation had regained stability on a permanent basis after the civil wars, then the young Tacitus may still have evolved into a very different kind of writer; or he may even not have embarked on a writing career at all. After all, children and the young can be extraordinarily robust in adversity, and even potentially devastating early experiences can be formative, without totally defining the adult that the child will become. One can compare here Esther Hautzig's *The Endless Steppe* (1968), an extraordinary memoir about how the author's wealthy Polish Jewish family was arrested by the Russians in 1941 and then removed to a labour camp in Siberia. The young Hautzig proves remarkably resilient, sometimes more so than the adults around her, and although the Siberian exile was an important part of her life, it did not take over her identity as an adult. Tacitus did not have to face anything as extreme as this, as far as we know. However, in general, if an early unsettling experience is then compounded by exposure to evocative dangers as an adult, then the impact on an individual is likely to fundamental. This 'doubling' of significant incidents will be relevant for our author's development.

When Tacitus embarked on his public life after arriving in Rome during Vespasian's principate, his prospects initially looked good, and his career certainly flourished under the Flavians, as he himself testifies with a slightly embarrassed shuffle:

I must concede that my career was launched by Vespasian, advanced by Titus, and still further promoted by Domitian.

Histories 1.1

1. Tacitus before 'History'

By AD 88, Tacitus, who had married into a good consular family (*Agricola* 9), had been awarded a praetorship, that is a senior magistracy which served as a stepping-stone to the most lofty administrative positions in the Roman imperial system, and he had also been given a prestigious priesthood (*Annals* 11.11). This was followed (AD 89-93) by an absence from Rome, holding some sort of government post abroad (*Agricola* 45), although the precise details of his appointment remain elusive. On the surface, his successful career looks like that of a favoured political insider, but such a close relationship with the centre of power came at a personal cost, particularly in the latter stages. His return to Rome, the heart of the imperial machine, in AD 93 was not auspicious. For Tacitus and his colleagues were dealing with an increasingly autocratic emperor, Domitian (AD 81-96), whose arrogant and heavy-handed conduct was stirring up deep resentment in aristocratic circles. In this context, Tacitus' passing comment about Nero (pondering a trip away from Rome) has resonances: 'The senate and leading men were uncertain whether he should be regarded as more frightening at a distance or before them' (*Annals* 15.36). Nero, like Domitian, stays in Rome, allowing no respite to the aristocracy. As Eprius Marcellus, one of the protagonists in Tacitus' historical narratives, is made to say with a down-to-earth twist, 'I pray for good emperors, but I take them as they come' (*Histories* 4.9). Domitian was an emperor who had to be taken as he came, and as we will see, he casts a long shadow over Tacitus' literary works.

Not everyone was prepared to be as *laissez faire* in their attitude to emperors as Eprius Marcellus. The governor of Upper Germany, Antonius Saturninus, even embarked on an unsuccessful rebellion in AD 89, but this only exacerbated Domitian's suspicions of anyone who disagreed with him. The biographical tradition tells stories of a paranoid emperor, who had the walls of the colonnades where he took his walks studded with the reflective stone phengite 'so that he might see in its brilliant surface a reflection of what was taking place behind him' (Suetonius *Domitian* 14); and (more famously), Domitian apparently used to spend hours by himself, catching flies and stabbing them with a sharp writing-stylus (Suetonius *Domitian* 3, Dio 66.9). Biography, particularly in the hands of Suetonius, is a genre which tends towards the sensational, but the fact that such stories were told and preserved is still revealing about contemporary perceptions of Domitian. Although some modern scholars have put forward revisionist interpretations of his principate, suggesting that the predominant impression in our literary sources of a 'reign of terror' is exaggerated, there is no doubt that the last three years (AD 93-6) of his principate saw executions among the aristocracy (Suetonius *Domitian* 10, Dio 67.3, 11-12). In this context, Pliny the Younger calls Domitian 'that most savage beast' (*Panegyricus* 48) and the satirist Juvenal talks of 'times of savagery, in which he deprived the city of bright and famous spirits, with impunity and with no avenger (*uindice nullo*)' (4.151-2). This last formulation involves some interesting word-play: the Latin word *uindex* means 'avenger', but it must also evoke the historical figure of Julius Vindex, that man who first instigated revolt against Nero in AD 68. Juvenal is indignant that no such figure presented himself to confront Domitian, whose abuses of power were, if anything, even worse than Nero's. Earlier in the same satire, Juvenal refers to the time when 'Rome was slave to a bald-headed Nero' (4.38), i.e. Domitian (who was notoriously sensitive about his thinning hair). If Rome under Domitian was now in the hands of another 'Nero', that must have had disturbing resonances for Tacitus. Was history about to repeat itself? Citizens with a strong sense of self-preservation must have been deeply worried about where this would all lead. Such questions were answered brutally when some members of Domitian's immediate entourage chose to take control of the situation themselves by assassinating him (with the co-operation of his wife) on 18 September AD 96.

That drastic step was all very well, but the conspirators had not thought through what they would do subsequently, and the situation looked alarmingly unsettled until the group approached the elderly ex-consul Nerva, who agreed to become emperor in Domitian's place (and whose age and status must have called up memories of the elderly Galba in AD 68). That was not the end of the instability, however. Domitian had actually been rather popular with the soldiers, who were not impressed by Nerva's appointment:

> As for his murder, the people were indifferent, but the soldiers were very deeply upset and at once tried to call him 'Divine'. They were prepared even to avenge him, except that they lacked leaders. Shortly afterwards, they achieved their end, after demanding most insistently that his murderers be punished.
>
> Suetonius *Domitian* 23

Such disgruntled troops were naturally a menace to national security, particularly since (after the accession of Galba in AD 68) it was an open secret that 'an emperor could be made elsewhere than in Rome' (Tacitus *Histories* 1.4). If the soldiers didn't like Nerva, then there were certainly other possible candidates for them to promote.

The situation was made more tense by the fact that Nerva (like the elderly Galba before him) had no children. Even if an emperor was not ideal, his offspring could create a sense of dynastic security for the future and reassure through the prospect of changes to come. In lieu of children, Nerva had to turn to adoption as the only way to defuse a potential civil war. As the political crisis deepened over the summer of AD 97, after a riot of the praetorians, the crack troops in Rome, Nerva adopted as his son and successor, Trajan, the governor of Upper Germany (October AD 97). This was the man who had suppressed the rebellion of Saturninus in AD 89 under Domitian. Trajan had good family connections and (crucially) was popular with the soldiers, but how much control over the whole situation Nerva really had is unclear. It must have been a tense time in Rome, and there was clearly a very chilling possibility that the empire might see a replay of the civil wars of AD 68-9.

Tacitus, who was serving as suffect consul (one of the chief magistrates in the Roman state) in AD 97, had an excellent vantage point over all this looming trouble. One of his duties that year was to deliver the funeral oration for Verginius Rufus, an elderly ex-consul, who had recently died after breaking his hip in a fall (Pliny *Letters* 2.1). Yet that was hardly likely to have taken Tacitus' mind off the potential chaos, since the honorand was famous for repeatedly being offered the principate by the soldiers before and during the civil wars of AD 68-9. Although Rufus refused their offers, he had left instructions that his restraint should be celebrated on his tombstone:

1. Tacitus before 'History'

Here lies Rufus, who, after Vindex had been defeated, liberated the imperial power, not for himself, but for his country.

Pliny *Letters* 6.10

It is striking that when the soldiers first pressed Rufus to take power, he had been governor of Upper Germany, the very same post currently held by Trajan. So the parallels between the past and the present must have been clear to Tacitus' listeners at the funeral, and no doubt brought home the fact that, if Trajan had not been offered imperial power, he could easily have taken it for himself. In the event, when Nerva died in January AD 98, power passed to his successor without any repetition of violence, but Tacitus must have seen the disturbing parallels between the events of his youth (Nero's principate followed by civil war) and the present (Domitian's principate followed by what could so easily have been civil war). It was only a matter of luck that history did not repeat itself more closely, but the latter years of crisis appear to have triggered or accelerated the creative process in Tacitus, already an accomplished orator and politician. At 42 years old, he had not yet published anything, but all that was about to change.

Tacitus' literary debut: the Agricola

One of the advantages of a first work is that nobody has any firm preconceptions about it, nor any expectations about its general character, genre or political stance. In AD 98, Tacitus was hardly a complete unknown – his skills as an orator had, after all, led him to be invited to deliver a prominent public oration at what was virtually a state funeral – but he still had relative freedom as a writer. So he was in an excellent position for capturing public attention, like anyone who is already well-known in one sphere and decides to embark on a venture in another area. One can think here of a figure like Martin Bell, the war correspondent, who put himself forward as an independent candidate in the British general election of 1997 in an attempt (successful, as it turned out) to oust the Conservative MP, Neil Hamilton. Bell's pre-existing prominence captured people's imaginations and made possible a success that would have been highly unlikely for an unknown challenger.

In the ancient world, Tacitus could have chosen from any number of genres for his literary debut, and he could have written in either prose or verse. What he produced in AD 98 was a politically provocative piece, difficult (to this day) to pigeon-hole in generic terms. The *Agricola* is ostensibly a biography of Tacitus' father-in-law Agricola (AD 40-93), about whom virtually nothing would be known if the work had not survived, but it is a much more ambitious and far-reaching piece than the simple label 'biography' would suggest (even if we concede that the ancient genre was rather different from its modern counterpart). The first oddity is that the *Agricola* is book-ended by a searing prologue (*Agricola* 1-3) and epilogue (*Agricola* 44-6), which denounce Domitian's oppressive principate and its deadly impact on the collective identity and spirit of the Roman aristocracy. If we compare the beginnings and ends of biographies written by Plutarch and Suetonius, there is nothing so morally hard-hitting and overtly rooted in recent history as this. Agricola's name is not even mentioned until the start of chapter 4, where Tacitus reverts to a more obviously biographical mode by presenting his father-in-law's family heritage. Indeed, if one did not know any better, and if by some accident of the manuscript tradition, chapter 4 had been presented as the start of the work, it would have felt like an appropriate opening. A similar point could be made about its close, if the narrative had finished at end of chapter 43. In fact, the discursive and outspoken prologue and epilogue of the *Agricola* seem highly reminiscent of a rather grander genre, the moralising openings of Sallust's historical monographs, the *Catiline* and *Jugurtha*, although even these provoked criticism from ancient readers: Quintilian, for instance, complains that these Sallustian prologues have nothing to do with the historical narrative that follows (*Training in Oratory* 3.8.9).

There are other peculiarities too that make the *Agricola* seem a slippery generic hybrid. Although we know that Agricola's life spanned 53 years, Tacitus elaborates one portion of it almost completely at the expense of everything else, namely his governorship of Britain (probably AD 78-84) under Domitian (*Agricola* 18-38). The campaigns of that period are described in a detailed way, on a year-by-year basis, in a manner highly reminiscent of another genre, annalistic history, as handled by the great Roman historian Livy. What with the focus on annual campaigning (*Agricola* 18-38) and within that, the provision of a grand battle narrative of the clash between Romans and Caledonians at Mons Graupius (*Agricola* 30-8), it feels as if we are reading traditional republican history, although with one crucial difference: Livian historiography conspicuously alternates between segments concentrating on military activities abroad, and those recording activities in Rome. Yet Tacitus, while actively recalling the genre of history, bastardises this familiar arrangement by remaining silent about events in Rome in the body of the work, although he will compensate for that in his focus on Domitian and Agricola (*Agricola* 39-43) after his father-in-law's departure from Britain. The overt nod to Livian historiography, but narrated with a twist, cleverly makes us think about Rome and wonder what is happening there, precisely because it is not mentioned. Silence can sometimes be extraordinarily expressive. Tacitus may choose to narrate Agricola's life in such a generically evocative and selective way precisely to maximise the contrast between the general's freedom in Britain and the politically oppressive climate in Rome. Yet it becomes clear as the biography unfolds that, despite the geographical distance between the province and the centre of power, Agricola (and his ilk) can never really extricate themselves successfully from the prevailing imperial ideology. The need for Roman readers (particularly those with public duties to fulfil) to associate themselves with Agricola also helps to explain another distinctive feature of the work: sometimes we have to remind ourselves that Tacitus actually knew Agricola personally, because the narrative is certainly not overwhelmed by the sort of exclusive and revealing anecdotes that this close family acquaintance would lead one to expect. Indeed, Agricola emerges from the narrative more as a general type than a unique individual. He serves as a sort of 'everyman', with whom contemporary readers can potentially identify, quietly getting on with his job and functioning as efficiently as possible under a totalitarian emperor. For Tacitus, that is far better than indulging in heroics and getting oneself killed. Indeed, it arguably mirrors what he himself did under Domitian, and thus serves as a form of self-defence by proxy.

Another generic 'import' is Tacitus' excursus on the geography and ethnography of Britain, placed prominently and relatively early in the life (*Agricola* 10-12). For some readers, this almost sets up 'Britain' as an independent character in the narrative in her own right, but whether or not one agrees with that sort of reading, it certainly recalls similar passages in Caesar's *Gallic War* (on the ethnography of the Gauls and Germans, *Gallic War* 6.11-28) and in Sallust's *Jugurtha* (on the geography and peoples of Africa, *Jugurtha* 17-19). Both works represent genres other than biography. Caesar wrote memoirs, purportedly designed to provide raw material for a continuous historical narrative, while Sallust produced a historical monograph. The extended ethnographical excursus that Tacitus provides in the *Agricola*, not generally a feature of ancient biography, therefore introduces a new element and recalls works associated with the republic, when foreign countries were seen as assets to be incorporated within the imperial structure and when ethnographical surveys were therefore a useful tool for understanding the potential conquest.

Everything that we have considered so far shows how eclectic and unusual the *Agricola* would have seemed to Tacitus' contemporaries. Yet it is the indignant and moralising prologue (*Agricola* 1-3) that signals particularly eloquently the innovative and far-reaching nature of this highly politicised little biography. Tacitus starts by establishing a set of polarities between the (implicitly republican) past and 'our age' (*nostra tempora*, *Agricola* 1), tarnished and crippled by comparison. In the past, Tacitus says, it was the custom to hand down to posterity the deeds and habits of famous men, and even now the practice has not totally disappeared from sight, whenever a worthy subject has managed to overcome those contemporary vices, ignorance of what is right (*ignorantia recti, Agricola* 1) and jealousy (*inuidia, Agricola* 1). The idea is cleverly formulated as a generalisation, but it will have particular resonance towards the end of the work, when Domitian withdraws Agricola from Britain, resentful that this talented general has made his own campaigns in Germany look hollow in comparison (*Agricola* 39). Yet the past was also more fruitful than the present, Tacitus argues, because writers willingly put themselves forward 'to hand down the memory of [their subjects'] valour' (*ad prodendam uirtutis memoriam, Agricola* 1), whereas now a biographer has to apologise in advance for celebrating his subject's achievements. Indeed, some biographers, such as Arulenus Rusticus and Herennius Senecio, even faced capital punishment for their works, which were publicly burned in the forum (*Agricola* 2). The vivid scene is like something from Ray Bradbury's futuristic dystopia, *Fahrenheit 451* (1953), which articulates the dangers of censorship in a totalitarian society (451°F is the temperature at which paper burns). Tacitus pours scorn on the perpetrators:

> Of course, by that fire they assumed that the voice of the Roman people, the liberty of the senate, and the awareness of humanity were being destroyed!
>
> *Agricola* 2

Yet his defiance flares only briefly, as he acknowledges wearily that 'we have certainly given (*dedimus*) substantial proof of our submissiveness; and even as former generations saw the best of liberty, so we (*nos*) have seen the low-point of servitude' (*Agricola* 2). Tacitus' use of the first-person plural is particularly intriguing here. Ancient writers striving for grandeur often used the first-person plural for effect, but its deployment now, in a pejorative context of admitting that contemporary society submitted to such oppression in the recent past, is significant. For Tacitus is not excluding himself from the wider group, who humiliatingly put up with the worst kind of servitude. In a contemporary audience, Tacitus surely provokes, not pride in having survived an oppressive regime, but shame that they tolerated it in the first place – and he is just as guilty as anyone else. This is confrontational writing indeed, addressing the troubles of the past just when many would rather simply move on and evasively look to the future. However, if anything good can come out of such oppression, Tacitus is determined that it should, and his prologue has a clear political purpose, in the sense that George Orwell meant it ('Why I Write', 1946):

> Using the word 'political' in the widest possible sense. Desire to push the world in a certain direction, to alter other people's idea of the kind of society that they should strive after.

While reading the prologue, we become aware that Tacitus' concept of 'now' is not static. Sometimes it has a general resonance, 'these days' as opposed to the more worthy past, but at other times it has a very specific sense, 'now' meaning AD 98, after the accession of Nerva apparently drew a line under Domitian's totalitarian regime: 'Now at last our spirit returns' (*Agricola* 3), even if in practice, 'you can stifle talents and enthusiasm more easily than revive them' (*Agricola* 3). It becomes clear that the apparently simple polarity between an outspoken past and oppressive present (with which the prologue opened) is much more nuanced. The crippled freedom of speech that

Tacitus associates with the present day, a legacy of Domitian's principate, need not stay that way, provided that his contemporaries make the most of their opportunity to heal themselves, but he also acknowledges that this will not happen automatically. Society is in a particularly precarious state:

> Given that, over fifteen years (a substantial span of a human life), many have fallen through chance happenings, while every most energetic man has perished by the emperor's savagery, the few of us left are, so to speak, survivors not only of the others, but of ourselves [*non modo aliorum, sed etiam nostri superstites sumus*], since so many years have been removed from the middle of our lives. During this time, our young men have become old, and our old men have almost reached the very boundaries of their lifespan, while we all kept quiet.
>
> *Agricola* 3

This is an extraordinary passage. What is especially intriguing is that it contains the first overt mention of Domitian: his principate is the implicit point of reference so far, whenever Tacitus refers to oppression, but we have to supply that context ourselves. It would have been so easy for Tacitus to engage in an extended polemic with the dead Domitian throughout this prologue (and indeed that will eventually come, in the narrative of Agricola's death), but instead, he explores the impact of that principate on the collective identity of the Roman aristocracy: fifteen years of silent acquiescence have turned the survivors into something different, very different from their former selves before Domitian came to power. Nothing can reverse that dreadful metamorphosis, but they do have control over their futures, and indeed a pressing obligation to record a harrowing past for posterity. Tacitus says that he 'will not regret commemorating the previous servitude and bearing witness to present blessings, however unpractised and rough my voice' (*Agricola* 3).

In this context, all of those odd generic twists in the body of the *Agricola* (such as the infiltration of ethnography and history) reinforce the idea (however disingenuous) that this work constitutes the halting efforts of an author trying to regain his voice after a stifling period of tyranny. For all we know, Tacitus had been quietly working away on his biography ever since his father-in-law's death in AD 93, but it was a brilliant stroke to publish the final version only in AD 98. By doing that, Tacitus powerfully endorses the fundamental image set up in the biography of Domitian's principate as a tyrannical twilight zone in which free speech (whether written or oral) was ruthlessly suppressed. To have published the *Agricola* any earlier would have undermined that model, because it would have suggested that the writing process had commenced while Domitian was still in power. Instead, Tacitus conveys a work bursting forth after a prolonged and enforced silence. James Cain does something rather similar in his novel *Serenade* (1937). In a story involving a famous opera singer who is forced to go on the run and stay in hiding after his wife has committed murder, Cain depicts the singer's distress at having to stay quiet, or risk detection:

Then I began to get this ache across the bridge of my nose. You see, it wasn't that I was thinking about the fine music that I couldn't sing any more, or the muted song that was lost to the world, or anything like that. It was simpler than that, and worse. A voice is a physical thing, and if you've got one, it's like any other physical thing. It's in you, and it's got to come out.

Just as the opera singer stopped performing to stay alive, Tacitus, whatever the reality, implies that he has exercised self-censorship over an extended period by not writing the *Agricola* while the tyrannical Domitian was in power, causing his 'voice' to grow rusty in the process. Now that the oppression has gone, however, he feels a compulsion to speak out at last. His purpose, apart from celebrating Agricola's achievements, is to demonstrate to posterity 'that there can be great men even under bad emperors' (*Agricola* 42). This is an interesting proposition, and one that suggests caution for the future: if Tacitus really had faith in the calibre of Trajan and his successors, why would a work demonstrating such a possibility even be necessary?

The *Agricola* closes, appropriately enough, with the death of its subject, but Tacitus adds an emotive coda (*Agricola* 44-6), triggered by his reflection that Agricola was actually lucky to die when he did (AD 93), because that meant that he did not see the worst excesses of the tyranny, when Domitian 'no longer drained the state of its blood fitfully and with breathing-spaces, but (as it were) with one constant blow' (*Agricola* 44). He painfully revisits the notion of collective guilt, ruthlessly piling on the first-person plurals, and reminding us of the prologue: 'Next our hands (*nostrae … manus*) dragged Helvidius to jail' (*Agricola* 45). He does not mean this literally, but in the sense that nobody, including himself, was able (or prepared) to stop such fatal victimisation from happening. Yet at the end of the biography, Tacitus becomes more reflective, and contrasts Agricola with many of

28

the worthy ancients, who have been forgotten because nobody recorded their lives for posterity. The very last sentence claims that, in contrast to such people, Agricola, 'whose story has been told and handed down to posterity, will be a survivor (*superstes*)'. Tacitus, himself one of the fragmented and crippled 'survivors of ourselves' (*Agricola* 3), but a consummate literary artist, has finally made sure that the dead Agricola too will be a 'survivor' and outlive the tyranny.

This is a remarkably defiant and complex way to end the biography. Tacitus does not deny or play down his own guilt in collaborating with a brutal regime, but he turns his own survival into something positive by salvaging something from the ruins. In fact, Tacitus even trumps his own sense of the idealised past by providing Agricola (through the *Agricola*) with precisely the sort of immortal fame that some of his republican predecessors were denied because nobody wrote about them. That speaks of Tacitus' supreme confidence both in his own abilities and in the reception of the biography. It is a powerful concluding move, which recalls the poet Horace's celebration of the 'marriage' of the brave man and the literary artist who celebrates his deeds, suggesting the perfect fusion of *actor* ('doer') and *auctor* ('author'):

> Brave men lived before Agamemnon, and many of them, but they are all unwept and unknown, oppressed by the unending night, since they lack a sacred bard.
>
> *Odes* 4.9.25-6

Without a Homer (or a Tacitus), heroic deeds are destined to be ephemeral and fleeting. So, preservation of memory becomes just as valuable as creating the memorable achievements in the first place.

Mapping the margins: the Germania

Tacitus had already shown his lively interest in geography and ethnography in his excursus on Britain (*Agricola* 10-12), but this curiosity was developed and expanded in his next venture, the *Germania*, also published in AD 98, as a reference in the text to Trajan's second consulship suggests (*Germania* 37). In many ways it is a very different sort of work from the *Agricola*, although we can see some of the same ideological and political concerns being played out in the narrative. Tacitus follows in the footsteps of a well-established literary genre in the ancient world, ethnography, consisting both of independent treatises and distinct portions of works in other genres. The *Germania* offers us an engaging ethnographical monograph, falling into two distinct halves: the first (*Germania* 1-27) surveys the habits and customs of the *Germani* as a whole, while the second part considers the colourful individual tribes and the differences between them (*Germania* 28-46). Unlike in the *Agricola*, there is no prologue, laying down an interpretative framework for the narrative, so we therefore have to extrapolate its significance from the text itself and from the contemporary literary and political scene.

There are some aspects of the work which on the surface seem rather escapist, such as his description of the Harii, who have black shields, dye their bodies, and choose dark nights for fighting their battles, inspiring terror by 'the shadowy horror of a ghostly army' (*Germania* 43). That snapshot might send a pleasurable shiver down the spine of a reader enjoying the work from the safety and comfort of Rome, but it is rather different from the *Agricola*'s chilling images of a monstrous Domitian spilling the life-blood of the city in an ecstasy of carnage. Of course, the narrative is not completely dominated by diverting descriptions. In an important passage, Tacitus characterises these tribes collectively as the most formidable enemy Rome has ever faced:

> Not the Samnite, not the Carthaginians, not Spain or Gaul, nor even the Parthians have admonished us more often: indeed the liberty of the Germans is more keen than the monarchy of Arsaces. For what else has the East cast at us than the slaughter of Crassus …?
>
> *Germania* 37

His focus here on German liberty (*libertas*), which has been a thematic thread running through the descriptions of individual tribes, is important. The immediate point of contrast is the subservient east, whose peoples, according to popular ancient conceptions of environmental determinism, had been rendered weak, passive and unwarlike by the intense heat in which they lived. Yet as with many ethnographic works, there is a broader point of comparison in play, namely the nationality of the author and his audience, whose members would bring to the text their own identity and customs, using the ethnographic descriptions of the German tribes as a 'mirror' to reflect light back on themselves, as modern scholars have pointed out. And what the Romans saw would not always be very comforting. Take, for instance, a general observation that Tacitus makes about the Germans' attitude to money:

> To loan money at interest and extend it into interest payments is unknown, and therefore it is prevented more effectively than if it had been banned.
>
> *Germania* 26

This is a distinctly odd thing to say about a people which has already been described as (for the most part) not using money at all, and tending instead to barter goods, rather than to pay for them (*Germania* 5). Indeed, it would be as bizarre as a modern author writing about contemporary British culture saying that people in the twenty-first century generally don't go to the shops and pay for goods by handing over cattle. Tacitus' real point is to make his readers think about themselves, since these laudable and innocent Germans, unlike the sophisticated Romans, are not gripped by avarice, which compels them to indulge in dubious practices such as usury. He will investigate this problem in more detail in a subsequent work:

> Meanwhile, a great mass of accusers fell upon those who were increasing their wealth by usury, contravening the dictator Caesar's law, by which a precautionary limit was imposed on credit and possession within Italy. This law had long been ignored, because public good is generally placed second to private advantage.
>
> *Annals* 6.16

The Romans may be running a huge empire, but with access to money and goods inevitably comes a downwards cycle of temptation, greed, and corruption. Calgacus, Tacitus' Caledonian chieftain in the *Agricola*, memorably called the Romans 'plunderers of the world' (*raptores orbis, Agricola* 30) in a speech before battle to rouse his troops. Such places offered another useful forum for Tacitus to articulate criticisms about his own people, without seeming to endorse the negative too overtly, but he was not the only writer to engage in such moral denunciation. The republican historian Sallust was the past master:

> Does anyone at all these days compete with his ancestors in uprightness and hard work, instead of in wealth and extravagance?
>
> *Jugurtha* 4

So when Tacitus describes the praiseworthy practices of the Germans, not dominated by greed, he implicitly harks back to a more innocent, pre-imperial past of the Romans, rather as Virgil does when he refers to the Capitoline hill in Rome, 'golden now, but once bristling with woodland thickets' (*Aeneid* 8.348). As the empire expands, other authors show similar pessimistic concerns about the deteriorating Roman national character, but Tacitus' voice is particularly insistent on this point, which becomes a powerful theme running though all of his surviving works, diverse and distinct though their different genres may be. Collective self-criticism is not Tacitus' only reason for embarking on this study, and indeed he is also prepared to censure the Germans at various points, but it does offer an interpretative context for the tone of some observations in the body of the work.

We have seen how describing the Germans enables Tacitus to make some telling implicit criticisms of the Romans by comparison, but even so, he could in theory have directed his ethnographical spotlight towards any number of different peoples on the margins with the same result. What was it about the Germans that made them so attractive as a subject? Ever since the incursions of the Cimbri at the end of the second century BC and the infamous massacre of Quinctilius Varus' three legions by Arminius in AD 9, the Germans had exerted a horrified fascination on the Romans, whose interest in such a work could thus be guaranteed, even at the end of the first century AD. More recently and relevantly, the emperor Domitian had engaged in campaigns in Germany, making war on the Chatti in AD 83, which prompted him to celebrate a triumph, commemorate the conquest of Germany on his coinage, and adopt the title 'Germanicus', which he then decreed as the new name for the month of September (Suetonius *Domitian* 13). These campaigns therefore constituted an important part of Domitian's efforts to lay claim to traditional martial prestige ideally associated with a Roman emperor. It may all seem a little ostentatious to us, but it was all part and parcel of the legacy of Augustus, under whom military achievement became an expected part of an emperor's remit, and it was not very different from (say) the emperor Claudius' exaggerated celebration of his (brief) participation in the invasion of Britain. Domitian was not Claudius, however, and as we have seen, Tacitus had already engaged in an intensely antagonistic relationship with the dead ruler, so the publication of the *Germania* can in some sense be seen as a continuation of that hostility. So, when Tacitus has Agricola modestly reporting his achievements in Britain at the end of his campaigns, he offers a highly-charged, negative version of Domitian's reaction to the news:

1. Tacitus before 'History'

Domitian was deeply aware that his recent sham triumph over Germany had become a source of mockery, after he had bought through deals men whose build and hair could be adapted so that they would appear to be captives.

Agricola 39

This story bears more than a passing resemblance to an incident associated with the emperor Caligula, who allegedly found some suitably tall Gauls, dyed their hair red, gave them German names, made them learn German, and allocated them to appear in a triumph for a war which had never even been fought (Suetonius *Caligula* 47). The nature of both scams has something in common with the memorable film *Capricorn One* (1978; jump to the end of this sentence if you have not seen it), in which a celebrated manned NASA expedition to Mars turns out to be based on an elaborate deception, cooked up after technical problems emerge, and reflecting the fact that American failure to excel in space would become a public-relations disaster. To return to the fake captives, the fact that a dubious story associated with one emperor appears to have been transferred (almost unchanged) to another emperor should perhaps make us suspect its validity. Perhaps it was just too good a weapon for Tacitus to pass up in the circumstances, although it is certainly true that other writers broadly cast aspersions on the campaigns. So, Pliny the Younger says that under Trajan, the Capitol will not receive 'fake chariots, nor illusions of a false victory, but a real commander' (*Panegyric* 16), although this is part of a series of polarities designed to celebrate Trajan and condemn Domitian. The Greek historian Dio also assesses the campaign negatively: 'he directed campaigns into Germany, and

35

not even having seen the war, he returned' (67.4.1). Perhaps Domitian's concerted and excessive exploitation of the war as a public-relations gambit, together with his later aggressive treatment of the aristocracy, meant that posterity would inevitably assess the campaigns in a hostile way.

Tacitus certainly continued his belittling of Domitian's efforts in the *Germania*:

> Most recently they [i.e. the Germans] have been the subjects of triumphs more than conquests.
>
> *Germania* 37

This sarcastic comment comes at the end of Tacitus' brief historical snapshot of interaction between the Romans and Germans over the past few centuries. It is conspicuous both for its brevity, particularly in comparison with the other phases of international relations that are described, and for its omission of any mention of Domitian by name. It almost feels like a literary enactment of *damnatio memoriae*, the punishment carried out by the senate, whereby an individual's name is thoroughly removed from inscriptions and his statues are destroyed (or at least the head removed). This served to 'blot out' that individual from the collective memory (even if it was often an important part of the disgrace that the gaps thereby created could still be seen). The emperor had indeed been formally punished after his death in this way (Suetonius *Domitian* 23), and it is significant that although Tacitus names Domitian eleven times in the *Agricola* (with references clustering particularly at the end of the work), there is not a single mention of his name in the *Germania*. To publish a detailed ethnographic study of the heterogeneous Germans (much of it in the present tense) in AD 98 was almost to suggest that Domitian's campaigns hadn't happened at all. The act of cataloguing and classifying the various tribes and mapping their terrain suggests that there is still much work to be done before these peoples are firmly brought into the Roman sphere. The ending of the work is particularly interesting in this regard. Tacitus finishes his account by mentioning the Hellusii and Oxiones, 'who have human faces and features, but the bodies and limbs of beasts. This, as something not yet ascertained, I shall leave open' (*Germania* 46). Ancient audiences loved to read about bizarre tribes beyond the margins of the known world, people such as the Panotii (literally 'All-Ears' in Greek), whose ears are so extensive that they can use them as clothes (Pliny *Natural History* 4.95), or the well-endowed men who float around on their backs using their penises as masts for sails (Lucian *True Histories* 2.45). Yet Tacitus' open-ended finale, with its focus on the exotic end of the ethnographic spectrum, is more than just straightforward entertainment. It raises a political question. What were Domitian's claims to have conquered Germany really worth, if there were still such bizarre and undocumented tribes out there, the fantasy stuff of myth, rather than the bread and butter of Roman imperial triumphs?

At the same time, Tacitus' rich ethnographical monograph, like the *Agricola*, was arguably not just a critique of the past, but a manifesto for the future. If the patchwork of tribes in Germany was still ripe for Roman intervention, then the man who would execute that operation was the new emperor, the militarily-oriented Trajan, still on the Rhine when the *Germania* was published. He had been appointed as governor of Upper

Germany in autumn AD 96 by Nerva, and although the two
great wars of conquest which took place in his principate would
be in Dacia and Parthia, that was all in the future when Tacitus
published the *Germania*. If Tacitus thought that Trajan might
direct his military attention to Germany, then the publication of
the *Germania* could serve to raise the profile of the area in
advance and to demonstrate that its proper incorporation in the
Roman empire would bring with it valuable resources and
lasting glory for the conqueror. It is pointed, for instance, that
when Tacitus indicates how long the attempted conquest of
Germany has been going on, he starts with the consulship of
Caecilius Metellus and Papirius Carbo in 113 BC and ends with
Trajan's second consulship in AD 98: 'that is the length of time
it is taking to conquer Germany' (*Germania* 37). Not only does
this formulation neatly efface all of Domitian's efforts in the
past, but it also makes clear that Germany has still not been
conquered, paving the way for a possible laudable intervention
in the near future by Trajan. This is not to say that Tacitus'
primary purpose in publishing the *Germania* was to influence
Trajan's imperial policy, but it may well have been an undercur-
rent within the work, which must have reflected contemporary
speculation in Rome about the possible character and direction
of the new principate. Clearly, if the text had not been an
engaging and well-researched ethnographical monograph in its
own right, capable of generating aesthetic pleasure and stirring
public interest, then any potential political impact would have
been swiftly undermined. Much the same can be said of Virgil's
epic poem, the *Aeneid*, since any potentially positive light cast
on the emperor Augustus would have been dim and short-lived
if the poem itself had lacked depth and complexity.

Finally, Tacitus himself was clearly fascinated by the German tribes and their shifting identities in relation to Rome, as we can see from his subsequent extended focus on two devious individuals, the Romanised Batavian rebel leader Julius Civilis in *Histories* 4 and 5 and the Cheruscan trouble-maker Arminius in *Annals* 1 and 2. Both these men, who had served as auxiliary leaders in the Roman army, are rather more tarnished and grubby at close hand than some of the idealised types of German we see from a distance in the *Germania*. As we will see, Tacitus' realistic portrayal of this pair of Germans shows that specific historical events and another genre (historiography) will require a very different narrative voice from the one adopted for the timeless and generalising ethnographical monograph.

Things ain't what they used to be? The Dialogus

Under the Roman republic, there were various ways to achieve personal glory and to serve the state simultaneously. For younger men, becoming a general was a crucial stage of any career, and the intrinsic value of professional military action was deeply embedded in the Roman psyche as a passport to renown. In fact, respect for military success was so central that problems inevitably emerged, once the empire had reached its optimum size and possibilities for conquest became more elusive (particularly since any glory acquired through military service was considered the exclusive reserve of the emperor). Tacitus' presentation of Agricola's career, abruptly curtailed through Domitian's jealousy, eloquently demonstrates this point, as do the personal stories of other talented generals, such as Domitius

Corbulo under Nero (narrated in the *Annals*) and Antonius Primus under Vespasian (narrated in the *Histories*).

According to Suetonius, Rome in the old days was such a warlike city-state that there was little time for anything else, including the study of grammar and oratory, which was not practised or held in honour (*On the Grammarians and Orators* 1). That changed, and increasingly the other way for aristocrats to achieve renown was through displaying their rhetorical skills, whether in the senate or in the law-courts. Words could often be just as effective a weapon as arms, and equally dangerous in the wrong hands. Roman society thus took rhetorical training seriously, so that it formed the bedrock of the aristocratic education, and boys engaged in elaborate rhetorical training exercises (conducted in the 'declamation schools') to prepare them for the cut and thrust of real legal cases. Speaking (and indeed writing) was ideally not something to be indulged in for its own sake and in a vacuum, but was seen as a means for an individual to give something back to the state. As the republican historian Sallust says:

> It is a fine thing to serve the state well by action, but even to speak eloquently on its behalf is highly appropriate.
>
> *Catiline* 3

If anything, the turbulent political conditions of the late republic meant that the services of oratory were widely deployed, and talented orators were sought after, as prolonged power struggles unfolded amongst the aristocracy. The deployment of invective and eulogy, whether in the law-courts, political pamphlets or senatorial debates, was one invaluable weapon in a more extensive war. The significance of political conditions for the 'health' of oratory is a point that Tacitus' Maternus explores in the context of the late republic:

> Although all these troubles racked the state, they nevertheless allowed the oratory of those days to flex its muscles and were seen to heap on it great rewards.
>
> *Dialogus* 36

Nevertheless, in the end violence will always trump eloquence, as we can see when the silver-tongued Cicero was brutally beheaded in 43 BC, while trying to escape from the soldiers carrying out the triumviral proscriptions. This was a period when Octavian, Lepidus and Antony drew up lists of 'enemies of the state' and posted rewards for the removal of their victims, who could not talk their way out of trouble, no matter how eloquent they were. The beheading of Cicero is a highly symbolic moment, full of unsettling resonances for the future of the Roman state.

The death-spasms of the republic and the evolution of the principate certainly spelled trouble for oratory. After the assassination of Julius Caesar, whose absolute power proved too much for his contemporaries to stomach, Augustus wisely exercised his ingenuity by casting himself as 'first among equals' and tinkering with the traditional mechanisms of authority. This created the comforting illusion that the principate was a co-operative venture between himself and the (now depleted) aristocracy, but all the while he was drawing real power firmly into his own orbit. Oratory had always thrived in the past because those who exercised it had a real stake in the power-structures, but things were now different. With power concentrated in the hands of one man, how could senatorial debate flourish, when members were constantly trying to second-guess the wishes of the emperor? Suetonius captures the sense of frustration:

> From time to time, as Augustus was rushing from the senate house in anger at the unrestrained and quarrelsome tone of the debates, some men shouted after him that he ought to let senators speak candidly about matters of state.
>
> *Augustus* 54

The situation only deteriorated after that. Even the recriminations of the emperor stopped, and Augustus' successor Tiberius habitually used to denounce senatorial sycophancy by saying in Greek every time he left the senate house, 'O! Men primed for slavery!' (Tacitus *Annals* 3.65). Things were not much better in the law-courts. Under the republic, jurisdiction lay with the magistrates, but it was now possible for appeals to be made to the emperor, and even for entire cases to be tried before him, which naturally placed the orators under great pressure. What they said could now get back to the emperor, whose intervention in their cases was always a real possibility. Finally, even in the private sphere, what you said could get you into desperate trouble, as treason by word as well as by deed became normal after Augustus. The atmosphere is vividly illustrated by Tacitus' infamous story of the 'senators in the ceiling', where one member of this once respected body tricks his victim into making negative remarks about the emperor, while three others listen in and denounce the man to Tiberius (*Annals* 4.68-9).

1. Tacitus before 'History'

The new power structure of the principate meant that oratory and free speech in general were under constant assault. It was not all the doing of the incumbent at the top, since pre-emptive sycophancy and self-censorship in society at large became endemic, but it all served to make more urgent the question of what purpose was to be served by rhetorical training and oratory in this altered political climate. Even the emperors themselves stopped bothering. Nero is said to be the first ruler to have needed 'borrowed eloquence' (*Annals* 13.3) and figures such as Otho's spin-doctor, Galerius Trachalus (*Histories* 1.90), became increasingly common. Why go through the tedious business of rigorous rhetorical training when you could just as easily buy somebody else's talents? Even if the speech was unconvincing, people would probably do what you wanted anyway.

This was the backdrop against which Tacitus composed his third work, the *Dialogus*, published perhaps in AD 101/2, but staged in AD 75, in the middle of Vespasian's principate. It takes the form of a debate between three principal speakers about the state of contemporary oratory, witnessed by Tacitus as a young man (although as a character in the work, he remains silent throughout). Curiatius Maternus is a lawyer and senator, an independent minded character, who is conspicuously turning his back on public life in favour of writing tragedies. Critics have seen some parallels between him and Tacitus, although the idea of reading him as a mouthpiece for Tacitus' own views is too crude. Maternus is quite prepared to defend his position and does so eloquently (*Dialogus* 11-14), even if he is totally unknown outside the *Dialogus*, just like his first interlocutor, Marcus Aper. He is another lawyer, a modern man, who begins the debate by enthusiastically advocating the merits of oratory over poetry (*Dialogus* 5-10), and who later defends the status of modern oratory over its older counterpart (*Dialogus* 16-23). He is a likeable figure, but he will ultimately be outweighed (and out-fought) by his two companions. The third character in the debate is a latecomer, Vipstanus Messalla, who comes from a well-established family with republican roots and who thinks that oratory in the past was better than it is now (*Dialogus* 25-6). He effectively 'wins' the first part of the debate, opening the way for the central concern of the work, an analysis of why oratory has declined. Messalla favours the explanation that standards of education have declined (*Dialogus* 28-35), while Maternus outspokenly blames the autocratic system of the principate, which strangles the opportunities for deploying rhetorical talents properly (*Dialogus* 36-41).

Tacitus was certainly not the first writer to tackle the subject of declining standards in contemporary oratory. So, Vespasian's professor of rhetoric, Quintilian, wrote a piece called *The Reasons for Debased Eloquence*, now lost, but published before the *Dialogus*, and the Neronian author Petronius provocatively denounces the state of contemporary oratory via his main character, Encolpius:

> Sorry to offend you rhetoricians, but let me say that it was you lot, who first of all ruined true eloquence. For by concocting ridiculous speeches through your trivial and hopeless prattling, you brought it about that the body of oratory lost its sinew and died.
>
> Petronius *Satyicon* 2

The perception that oratory had died with the republic, in particular with Cicero, finds expression relatively early in the

principate. The historian Velleius Paterculus, who lived under
Tiberius, notices the phenomenon, although (unlike Tacitus'
interlocutors in the *Dialogus*) he is at a loss to explain why it
followed this trajectory:

> As for forceful forensic oratory and the sublime splendour of
> eloquence in prose … it all burst forth under Cicero, the
> master of the genre, in such a way that you can take delight in
> very few of its exponents before him, and indeed you can
> admire nobody except men who had either seen Cicero or
> been seen by him.
>
> *History of Rome* 1.17

In the light of such gloomy assessments, perhaps the most
remarkable point about Tacitus' *Dialogus* is that any of the interlocutors even bothers to argue that contemporary rhetoric had
not declined, but given that Tacitus himself was a practising
orator, the thesis about deteriorating standards that emerges by
the end of the work still seems pretty nihilistic.

As often, however, views in Tacitus' narrative are not as
certain or static as they might at first appear. There are indica-
tions outside the text that concerned and talented men were
trying to address the problem. So, under Vespasian, Quintilian
wrote an extensive work, the *Training in Oratory*, which ad-
vocated a return to Ciceronian standards of oratory after the
perceived rhetorical excesses of the Neronian era, and which laid
down ways for the creation of the morally robust 'good man
skilled at speaking' (*uir bonus dicendi peritus,* 12.1.1). Even
Tacitus' pessimism is complicated by the fact that his thesis is
articulated in a work which so obviously displays the talents of

a skilled rhetorician, rather as Virgil's famous sharp contrast (*Aeneid* 6.847-53) between stodgy, bureaucratic Romans and arty, expressive Greeks is mischievously deconstructed by the beautiful poem in which the observation is lodged. Under the principate, prestige gained by literary activities was swiftly becoming a useful third way to achieve renown, alongside (or even over and above) the traditional and increasingly debased routes by oratory and martial activity. Tacitus may decry the state of contemporary oratory, but the *Dialogus* offers him an alternative or additional medium for displaying his own talents (and it may also be relevant that the debate is set in AD 75, rather than under Trajan).

There are signs of life too in the fact that Tacitus' younger contemporary, Pliny the Younger, ardently believed that it was above all through his oratory that he would secure his post-humous fame. During the principate, traditional avenues to glory were (by necessity) under reconstruction, but, as Roland Mayer has argued, Pliny actively tries to reinstate his own oratory as a mechanism for creating glory. He did this by publishing both his speeches themselves and complementary letters, which can engagingly flesh out the context of a speech's delivery and pique general interest. That Pliny's forensic speeches have not survived where his letters have done so is more likely to reflect the accidents of manuscript transmission that the calibre of the oratory.

It is rare, perverse even, to characterise the *Dialogus* as in some sense an optimistic work, but the fact that under Trajan, Tacitus is able to publish a discussion which so obviously suggests a link between the prevailing ideology of the principate and the flawed state of contemporary oratory at least indicates some progress. To deny a problem or pretend that it does not exist can only exacerbate it, but the *Dialogus*, with its conversational style and enagagingly urbane characters, serves to open up a healthy public debate. That may be prompted by Tacitus' rather open-ended closural strategy in the last chapter of the work. After Maternus has finished his final speech, Messalla says that there are points which he would like to take up, but concedes that it is getting late. Maternus replies:

> 'We will discuss these details later, whenever you please. If any points in this discourse of mine seemed baffling to you, we will talk about them again.'
>
> *Dialogus* 42

The *Dialogus* is hardly an excessively lengthy work, and Tacitus could surely have postponed the conventional closural device of the day's end to include another pair of speeches, or even two. The fact that he does not do so, while at the same time indicating that the debate is far from finished, is surely encouraging his own readers to pick up where internal speakers left off. They may in the end conclude that Maternus and Messalla are right about the state of contemporary oratory, but in discussing the problem amongst themselves, they are at least beginning to do something positive about it. And there is always the possibility that some may endorse Aper's more optimistic stance. As Tacitus says elsewhere:

> Not everything was better among our predecessors, but our era too has generated many laudable achievements in the arts, which are worthy of imitation by posterity. In any case,

let the results of these contests with our ancestors achieve lasting honour.

Annals 3.55

The immediate context for this comment (itself digressive) is a digression on why luxurious standards of living became less prominent after the civil wars of AD 68-9, but in stepping back to acknowledge the potential for the artistic achievements of the Trajanic present to be imitated by posterity, Tacitus suggests that significant areas of contemporary creativity, literature and perhaps also oratory (at least published speeches), now have a very decent claim to excellence in their own right. That view coheres with the relatively optimistic and open-ended reading of the *Dialogus* suggested here.

Conclusion

The *Agricola*, *Germania* and *Dialogus* show Tacitus to be a hugely versatile writer with formidable literary talents, more than ready to be exercised in works on a grand scale in a genre right at the top of the literary hierarchy. Tacitus' early works can be read independently, but they also form a kind of triptych, each in different ways interrogating contemporary Roman identity under the principate and probing the collective health of the Roman state. They are all moralising studies, steeped in a pessimistic awareness of decline, but at the same time they show Tacitus edgily opening up debates with his contemporaries and trying to shake them from a state of lethargy, which for many had become a 'default mode' for survival under an oppressive regime. It is a brilliant stroke that by choosing to publish his works when he did, in AD 98 and beyond, he effectively endorses the damning image of Domitian's tyrannical principate shaped within the body of these texts.

One crucial point about these early works which also defines them is their style: we can see throughout how Tacitus experiments and plays creatively with his Latin, so that fundamental meaning is often enhanced by grammar, syntactical arrangement and choice of vocabulary. His readers ideally have to be alive to linguistic nuances and intellectually engaged with their own literary heritage, if they are going to get the most from these texts.

So, for example, at the start of the Caledonian rebel-leader Calgacus' speech, Tacitus clearly alludes to the opening of Cicero's speech *For Marcellus*, delivered in 46 BC and celebrating the restoration of one of Julius Caesar's old enemies, Marcus Marcellus. Where Calgacus emotively emphasises that 'today [*hodiernum diem*] will be the beginning of liberty for all Britain' (*Agricola* 30), the language evokes Cicero: 'today [*hodiernus dies*] has brought the end of my long silence' (*For Marcellus* 1). Both authors use the highly unusual periphrasis *hodiernus dies* instead of the more pedestrian term *hodie*. Yet many critics have characterised Cicero's whole speech for Marcellus as distastefully sycophantic and obsequious with regard to Julius Caesar (an imperial prototype, if ever there was one), so if Calgacus recalls it when calling his people to fight for liberty, it makes his point about the value of impending liberty all the more telling. Cicero, after all, lived under the republic, and if even he succumbs to servility, think how much worse the Romans are now and how crucial it is for the Britons to assert their independence from such oppressive masters.

Of course, Tacitus' text is perfectly understandable on one level without acknowledging the Ciceronian allusion. Yet it makes the experience of reading more provocative and absorbing if we stop to consider what the significance of this echo might be (and often there is not one easy, convenient answer in such cases). This sort of meaningful allusive 'layering' does not, on the whole, mirror the ways in which we tend to read (or write) today, but it is a crucial aspect of the higher branches of literature in the ancient world, particularly epic and historiography. This essential fusion between style and meaning will go on to become a distinctive and engaging aspect of Tacitus' historical narratives, as we will see.

If by some twist of fate, Tacitus' historical works had been completely lost, would his posthumous reputation have been secured by the *Agricola, Germania* and *Dialogus*? Or would Tacitus' 'minor works' be consigned to the margins of (what the modern world considers as) the canon of Classical texts? We can play this sort of game with any author who moved up the hier-archy of genres to produce mature works which went on to become more famous and widely read than the earlier works; and the answer is inevitably subjective to some extent. Virgil and Ovid are cases in point, or (to add a more recent example), the director Alfred Hitchcock, whose early films of the 1920s and 1930s are on the whole overshadowed by his later work in Hollywood from 1940 onwards. Or, as fellow-director François Truffaut put it diplomatically to Hitchcock: 'With the passage of time, those of us who have followed your overall career have the feeling that it was only after your arrival in the United States that you reached your creative peak.' Tacitus' own creative peak certainly came with his historiographical masterpieces, the

1. Tacitus before 'History'

Histories and the *Annals*, but it is probably fair to say that if we did not have access to these works, then the *Agricola, Germania* and *Dialogus* would be much more widely read today than they often are. In this sense, Tacitus is the victim of his own success.

2

The Peak of Creativity:
Tacitus' *Histories* and *Annals*

Introduction

Even while Tacitus was putting the finishing touches to the
Dialogus, he must have been contemplating the nature of his
next project. There is a hint as early as the *Agricola* that he was
aiming at a historical narrative as the culmination of his literary
career. So, at the end of the prologue, he says that he 'will not
regret [*pigebit*] having commemorated [*memoriam ... composu-
isse*] the previous servitude and bearing witness to present
blessings, however unpractised and rough my voice. This book
meanwhile [*interim*] ...' (*Agricola* 3). The future tense of the
verb and the emphasis on the *Agricola*'s interim status as a step
along the way to another (unspecified) project suggests that
even in this first work, Tacitus was carefully plotting for himself
an ambitious literary trajectory. His focus on *memoria*
('commemoration') calls to mind above all the memorialising
and monumental genre of historiography, which Quintilian
characterises as being written 'to preserve a memory for
posterity [*ad memoriam posteritatis*] and to enhance the fame of
its author' (*Training in Oratory* 10.1.31); and his references to
previous servitude and present blessings suggests the principates
of Nerva and Trajan as his likely focus.

2. The Peak of Creativity

Writing history was not something ideally to be undertaken early in a career, when an author was still earning his credentials. It was after all a genre which made exceptional demands on its practitioners, who required a certain authorial *auctoritas* ('authority') to carry it off successfully. As well as needing to research and collate the facts preserved by different pre-existing narratives, the budding historian had to choose an appropriate period of history to write about in the first place (not as easy as it sounds), develop an appropriately authoritative Latin style (which could vary tremendously, depending on the nature of the historical project), and breathe new life into the potentially hackneyed set-pieces of the genre, such as battle-narratives, sacking of cities and extended speeches. The early imperial historian Livy refers to

> ... the steady stream of new writers, who believe either that they will supply something more reliable in their facts or that they will outdo hoary antiquity in their style of writing.
>
> *From the Foundation of the City*, preface 2

Livy, artfully deploying a modesty *topos* (literary convention) to capture his readers' good-will, is apparently anxious that he will be in their number, either through flawed content or style (or both). In addition to such pressures, historiography was also a competitive genre, whose practitioners often tried to enhance the credentials of their own efforts by pouring scorn on the work of their predecessors. Polemical sallies, whether in general terms or against named individuals, are not uncommon. So, Tacitus questions the validity of a detail relayed by the Neronian historian Fabius Rusticus, 'who inclines towards praise of

Seneca, by whose friendship he flourished' (*Annals* 13.20), and Quintilian says laconically, but expressively, 'historians often disagree with each other' (2.4.19). He may have been thinking of infamous cases such as Polybius (a Greek historian of Rome, who flourished in the second century BC), whose extensive and ruthless critique of his predecessor Timaeus survives amongst the fragments of his history (*Histories* 12).

No wonder the genre did not appeal to every writer. It is striking, for example, that Pliny the Younger, who was a professional orator like Tacitus himself, shies away from writing history because he regards the genre as a minefield of difficulties (*Letter* 5.8). His refusal comes, despite the fact that it was part of his family tradition. His prolific uncle, Pliny the Elder, certainly wrote history, but we can see from his nephew's chronological survey of his works that the *History of the Wars in Germany* in twenty books comes only after a technical manual on the art of throwing a javelin from horseback and a biography of Pomponius Secundus (*Letter* 3.5). Writing history was not for a novice. It took considerable time and energy, and if a writer had any concerns about his reputation, he would be well advised to try his hand at 'lesser' genres first.

Moreover, contemporary critics could certainly be ruthless about attempts to innovate within this lofty genre, as Aulus Gellius makes clear when discussing the republican historian Sallust:

> Sallust's elegant style and his enthusiasm for coining and introducing new words certainly encountered much hostility, and many men of considerable talent tried to criticise and disparage various aspects of his writings.
>
> *Attic Nights* 4.15

2. The Peak of Creativity

Even busy emperors found time to read history, although they sometimes reacted in a hostile way on aesthetic or political grounds. Thus Caligula almost decides to have Livy's history removed from the libraries on the grounds that he was 'wordy and careless' (Suetonius *Caligula* 34). Livy was safely dead by that point, but another historian, Hermogenes of Tarsus, was not so lucky when Domitian was offended by some innuendoes in his historical work and executed him; and even the slaves who had copied out the manuscript were crucified (Suetonius *Domitian* 10). With these efforts to police the very mechanisms of book production, we might compare the Communist party in the Soviet Union in the 1930s, when the 'Goskomizdat' (State Committee for Publishing Houses, Printing Plants, and the Book Trade) made all publishing decisions, and even the allocation of paper became a hidden censorship mechanism.

The potential dangers of the profession under the emperors was not lost on Tacitus himself. A particularly memorable sequence from the *Annals* (4.34-5) involves the historian Cremutius Cordus, who was forced to suicide in Tiberius' principate for writing positively in his historical narrative about the 'tyrannicides', Brutus and Cassius, who had plotted to kill Julius Caesar, thus raising an ugly precedent for the emperors who followed in his wake. Tacitus puts in Cordus' mouth a lively and defiant defence about the pointlessness of trying to suppress freedom of speech, but even so, according to Quintilian, Vespasian's professor of rhetoric, the contentious passages have still not been restored to the text in his own day (10.1.104). So those writing history under the empire not only ran the familiar risk of meeting a hostile reception from critics, they were also pouring their talents into a genre which (in the worst-case scenario) had the potential to be lethal.

So why did talented and creative writers bother with the genre at all? An enticing incentive for many lay in the possibility of earning enduring fame through their writing. Every Latin author hoped that his written legacy, whatever the genre, would serve as a route to immortality. A particularly expressive articulation of this aspiration comes at the end of Ovid's *Metamorphoses*, an innovative epic poem in fifteen books:

> Now I have carried out my work, something which neither the anger of Jupiter, nor fires, nor sword, nor devouring age will be able to destroy. Let that day, which has no claim except over this body, end the span of my uncertain years when it wishes. I, however, or the finer part of me, will be carried high above the stars, to last forever, and my name will be indestructible. Wherever Roman might extends through the lands beneath her control, I will be read on the lips of the people and will be famous through all the ages, and if the predictions of the prophets have any truth, I will live.
>
> *Metamorphoses* 15.871-9

Over the course of this short, bullish epilogue, Ovid the mortal man undergoes a metamorphosis into 'Ovid' the immortal book, confident at escaping the clutches of all destructive forces, including the 'anger of Jupiter' (which many see as a gloss on the emperor Augustus, or indeed any future emperor who might take offence at Ovid's poem), and anticipating that the 'vehicle' of the (Latin-speaking) empire will be the means to his immortality. He also alludes to the famous epitaph of Ennius (239-169

BC), the respected 'grandfather' in many areas of Latin literature, who overtly laid claim to immortality through his writings: 'I flit through and live in the mouths of men' (preserved at Cicero *Tusculan Disputations* 1.34).

It may seem rather alien to us these days, but a desire to earn eternal fame triggered the creative process for many ancient writers. They were not bashful about candidly stating this hope, as does Pliny the Younger, when he considers the tempting possibility of writing history, which is a desirable genre because it can facilitate 'extending the fame of others, as well as one's own' (*Letter* 5.8). Yet even in the modern era, writers are often motivated by this factor, whether or not they are candid about it. At least this is what George Orwell thought, when he identified 'sheer egoism' as one of the four factors which makes people write. He defines it as follows:

> Desire to seem clever, to be talked about, to be remembered after death, to get your own back on the grown-ups who snubbed you in childhood, etc., etc. It is humbug to pretend this is not a motive, and a strong one. Writers share this characteristic with scientists, artists, politicians, lawyers, soldiers, successful businessmen – in short, with the whole top crust of humanity. The great mass of human beings are not acutely selfish. After the age of about thirty they almost abandon the sense of being individuals at all – and live chiefly for others, or are simply smothered under drudgery. But there is also the minority of gifted, wilful people who are determined to live their own lives to the end, and writers belong in this class. Serious writers, I should say, are on the whole more vain and self-centred than journalists, though less interested in money.
>
> 'Why I Write'

More mischievously, the American author Flannery O'Connor defined a writer as 'a fool, who, not content with having bored those who have lived with him, insists on tormenting generations to come'. This self-centred ethos which drives the talented (or untalented) to write finds precedents in the ancient world, although for the writing of history there is another important motivating factor for Roman authors, which qualifies Orwell's general characterisation of the profession in the modern world. Hand-in-hand with the desire to promote one's own undying fame by writing history goes the (more selfless) notion that the genre was a way to monumentalise and preserve for posterity the fame of others. A vibrant sense of the past (and more specifically the big personalities of the past) as shaping the present was a fundamental part of the Roman national character. So, the aristocracy proudly celebrated this dynamic within their own families by displaying in the entrance halls of their houses the wax portrait-masks of their dead ancestors, which were even brought out for public display at the funerals of these men's descendants. And as we have seen, distinguished orators such as Tacitus would be asked to deliver funeral laudations at the deaths of great men such as Verginius Rufus (Pliny *Letter* 2.10). Nor did the Romans consign to oblivion national disgraces, but discreetly kept them 'alive' as a warning to contemporary society. Accordingly, when the short-lived emperor Vitellius decided to take up the principate on 18 July AD 69, this prompted widespread public condemnation because that date was the anniversary of the Roman defeats at the battles at Cremera (*c.* 479 BC) and Allia (*c.* 387 BC) and had therefore been designated as an 'unlucky day' (*infaustus dies,* Tacitus *Histories* 2.91) when business was not conducted. This left time for quiet reflection about disastrous events in the past, which could so easily have prevented the Roman state from developing into the powerful empire that it eventually became. The modern equivalent (if it existed) would be to designate as an annual public holiday the anniversary of (say) the decisive and humiliating defeat of the English by the French at the battle of Formigny on 15 April 1450, which led to the French recovery of Normandy. Yet such a commemoration of the battle (imposed from above) would seem odd to a Roman observer, in that significant dates in their own history (even from the distant past) did not need such formal recognition in the calendar to retain their meaning. It was rather that the calendar reflected a collective awareness of the past that already existed in society. The concept of 'Lest We Forget' (appropriated from Rudyard Kipling's poem of 1897, *Recessional*, and applied to Remembrance Sunday, marking the anniversary of the end of the First World War) would have seemed alien indeed to the Roman mentality. Forgetting was out of the question.

The landscape of the past was, for the Romans, very much alive, and written history, just as much as physical monuments, funeral speeches and wax portrait-masks, was an invaluable way to preserve and shape the collective memory. For, as Cicero says, 'history ... is the lifeblood of memory' (*About the Orator* 2.36). Closely connected with this notion is the phenomenon of 'exemplarity', whereby cogent examples of individuals from history, whose conduct is to be emulated or avoided, were preserved for posterity. Livy plays up this valuable function of history in his preface:

This especially is what renders the study of history beneficial and fruitful, that you look upon the teachings of every kind of example, laid forth in an illustrious 'monument'.

From the Foundation of the City, preface 10

Ancient historiography, conceptualised by Livy architecturally as a physical monument, allows readers to see for themselves the useful lessons of the past, and thus improves the 'health' of the state. Tacitus' *Agricola* (in many respects a 'dry-run' for history) is driven by this same concern, as he preserves the story of one man, who will become a model for subsequent generations, after his story has been 'narrated and handed down to posterity' (*Agricola* 46). Writing history in the Roman world was therefore a well-established public duty, to be undertaken even when the prevailing political system made the process of memorialising difficult, or even dangerous. It was a genre deeply and urgently rooted in the present and the future, as well as in the past, and in this sense, it is rather a different beast from its modern counterpart.

In order to implement this 'exemplarity', ancient historiography had an overtly moralising agenda, which can seem strange to modern audiences. We get a good sense of this from a fragment of a republican historian, Sempronius Asellio, who lived in the second century BC, and discusses the differences between bare 'annals' and real history:

For books of annals are not able to make people any keener to defend the state or more reluctant to do wrong. Writing in whose consulship a war was started and finished, who as a result entered the city in triumph, and in that book not to explain what was done in the war, nor to say meanwhile what the senate decreed, nor what law or bill was passed, nor according to what advice these things were done – that is story-telling for children, not writing history.

Aulus Gellius Attic Nights *5.18*

Entertainment was all very well (and indeed those reading histor-ical narratives in the ancient world would certainly expect to get some aesthetic pleasure from the experience), but that is only a means to an end, namely the implementation of a serious moral-ising agenda, which would improve the state of the author's contemporary world. To borrow some terminology from ancient literary theorists, history had to be *utile* ('useful') as well as *dulce* ('enjoyable'). Tacitus' most famous predecessors in the genre, the republican historian Sallust and the early imperial historian Livy, were both well aware of that dual requirement, even if they found differing ways of putting it into practice.

Fall ... The Histories

If Tacitus wanted to initiate himself gently in the challenging profession of the historian, then he certainly picked a perverse and peculiar topic for his first work, the *Histories* (published probably in AD 109). It begins (paradoxically) with an ending, the aftermath of the demise of the Julio-Claudian dynasty, and starts (misleadingly) with a false beginning, the seizure of impe-rial power by Galba in AD 68, and follows his attempt to establish a new imperial dynasty, which was terminated brutally when he was decapitated by soldiers in the forum in Rome on 15 January AD 69. Tacitus' provocative playfulness with beginnings and endings is reflected in the fact that he opens formally by naming the consuls for AD 69 (a traditional chronological marker in annalistic history), then gives a preview of his subject-matter (*Histories* 1.2-3) and offers a chronological retrospective and geographical survey (*Histories* 1.4-11), only to revert in a circular way to the names of the consuls for AD 69 once again at the start of *Histories* 1.12. The narrative then covers the civil wars of AD 68-9 (dominating books 1-3 of the *Histories*), fought sequentially between the four emperors Galba (16 June 68 – 15 January 69), Otho (15 January 69 – 17 April 69), Vitellius (19 April 69 – 20 December 69) and Vespasian, and moves on to present the Flavian dynasty, namely the principates of Vespasian (AD 69-79), and his two sons Titus (AD 79-81) and Domitian (AD 81-96). Unfortunately, we now have just the first four books and part of the fifth, taking the story only as far as AD 70.

So, despite having the entire sweep of Roman history, from the traditional foundation of the city in 753 BC onwards, available as potential subject-matter, Tacitus opts to write about an uncomfortably recent period, some of whose central protagonists were still alive to take issue with his version of events. As Pliny the Younger says, when rejecting the genre of history for himself, if you choose to write about recent times, 'the potential for being offensive is grave, the opportunity to give pleasure is fleeting', particularly since 'amidst such vast human corruption, more elements must be censured than praised' (*Letter* 5.8). The potential for 'getting it wrong', and promptly being confronted with irate eye-witnesses prepared to give their 'true' version of events, was therefore considerable.

Yet at the same time, the contemporary nature of the topic also gave Tacitus access to a unique wealth of information, in the form of biographies, histories, general's memoirs, and the oral tradition, all of which must have allowed him to check stories about specific events against each other. We have evidence external to the text that Tacitus was actively engaged in this sort of meticulous research, as we can see from two letters of Pliny the Younger, written in response to Tacitus' request for information about the dramatic death of his uncle in the devastating eruption of Vesuvius in AD 79 (*Letters* 6.16, 6.20). Pliny is grateful to be asked, precisely because he feels confident that, if Tacitus writes about Pliny the Elder's death, then 'immortal glory' (*Letter* 6.16) will be the result for his uncle. It is ironic indeed that Tacitus' own version of the eruption has not survived, and that the enduring fame of Pliny the Elder's death has been created through Pliny the Younger's own account in the 'lesser' genre of epistolography. Yet the ancient world is riddled with such twists of fate.

We also have evidence from within the text that Tacitus has investigated the facts painstakingly. So, at one point, he highlights a discrepancy in his sources about which Flavian commander used the dubious incentive of pointing to the northern Italian city of Cremona as plunder to get the soldiers to fight more energetically: Pliny the Elder gives one name, and Vipstanus Messalla (the interlocutor of the *Dialogus*) provides another (*Histories* 3.28). This wealth of detail is a long way from (say) Livy's frustration at the dearth of sources available for the early history of Rome: he complains bitterly that literature was scant in those days, and that even so, any written records that did exist were burned when the city was sacked by the Gauls in 390 BC (*From the Foundation of the City* 6.1). Tacitus, if anything, has the opposite problem as a result of choosing such a recent period of history, particularly one incorporating the civil wars of AD 68-9, when propaganda surrounding the individual emperors was flying around thick and fast. The Greek writer Josephus apologises for not offering a comprehensive account of the civil wars, and concludes that

> I must excuse myself from describing any of these events in detail, because they are matter of common knowledge and have been dealt with by many Greek and Roman writers.
>
> *Jewish War* 4.495-6

The problem is particularly relevant today. As the media for preserving information multiply, the challenge of imposing clarity and meaning on events becomes ever more acute; and of course, the potential for complete falsification of evidence is just as great, as is clear from notorious cases such as Konrad Kujau's forgery of the Hitler Diaries in 1983. Likewise, in the civil wars of AD 68-9, there are hints that falsified documents were being deployed. For example, Suetonius mentions a letter (possibly a forgery) from the dead emperor Otho requesting that Vespasian (now the imperial challenger) should avenge him, and expressing his hopes that Vespasian would come to the aid of the state, i.e. become emperor (*Vespasian* 6). For what it is worth, Vespasian's own son, Titus, was supposed to have been a talented forger, capable of imitating anyone's handwriting (Suetonius *Titus* 3), though whether he had a personal hand in Otho's 'letter' is anybody's guess. At any rate, any historian writing about this period had to consider carefully the provenance of his documentary evidence.

Tacitus is well aware that not all of his readers will find his comparatively recent subject-matter attractive. Some are likely to be ambivalent because the account will cause them personal distress by reminding them of events which they would quite simply rather forget, while others could easily dismiss it as being just too barren a field for germinating the sort of uplifting narrative traditionally associated with Roman historiography. The need to persuade potentially hesitant or hostile readers to persevere with the *Histories* is therefore urgent, so as soon as possible, Tacitus provides a colourful overview of his prospective work to hook any waverers:

> I approach a work rich in disasters, fierce in battles, riven with seditions, brutal even during peacetime itself. Four emperors slaughtered by the sword, three civil wars, several foreign conflicts often mixed together with them. Things went well in the east, but disasters struck in the west; Illyricum was in chaos, Gaul was tottering, Britain was conquered, but immediately abandoned, the Sarmatian and Suebian peoples rose against us, the Dacians had the honour of defeating us and being defeated in turn, war even from the Parthians was almost triggered, thanks to the absurd sham of a false Nero. Now indeed Italy was afflicted with new disasters, or troubles revisited after a long period of years. Cities were swallowed into the earth or buried from above along the rich coast of Campania; and Rome was devastated by fires, while the most ancient temples were destroyed, with the very Capitol burnt down by the hands of citizens. Sacred rites were grossly profaned; there was adultery amongst the great. The sea was full of exiles, cliffs were stained with blood. The savagery in the city was still fiercer. Nobility, wealth, honours passed over or adopted, were taken as a crime, and good qualities

absolutely guaranteed death. The prizes granted to informers were no less hateful than their crimes, since some gained priesthoods or consulships as their spoils, while others won administrative posts and power at the very core, and their actions turned everything upside down with the hatred and fear they provoked. Slaves were bribed against their masters, freedmen against their patrons; and those without an enemy were ruined by their friends.

Histories 1.2

As a form of 'trailer' for the main feature, this is high-octane stuff, and it is artfully done. After the general opening, Tacitus sets in place a conspicuous centripetal momentum, moving briskly from events around the empire, to a sweeping view of trouble within Italy, and culminating in devastation at the centre in Rome itself. The sheer pace of the narrative style is extraordinary, with items placed paratactically (side-by-side without subordinate clauses or connectives), jostling for attention and with frequent ellipse of verbs (or parts of verbs) to accelerate the pace. The syntax and subject-matter creates a breathtaking sense of speed and dynamism, so that almost before you know it, you are completely immersed in the story, hungry for the next detail.

As a broad organisational strategy, Tacitus uses a loose chronological progression, starting with the main facets of the civil wars in AD 68-9, but also offering snapshot 'previews' of infamous events such as the eruption of Vesuvius in AD 79 ('Cities were swallowed ...') and the sexual scandal involving the Vestal virgins during the principate of Domitian, which resulted in one of them being buried alive as a punishment

('Sacred rites were grossly profaned ...'). The tone throughout is hyperbolic and attention-grabbing, with Tacitus using generalising plurals, although in several instances he is probably only referring to a single event. That is a technique more usually associated with the sensationalising narrative of the biographer Suetonius, but then again, this is an unusual section of Tacitean narrative, deliberately designed to draw us into the story, so exaggeration is called for.

It is also highly effective that all of this is relayed in inventive and innovative Latin, full of rich metaphors and striking poeticisms. I know that not everyone reading this study of Tacitus will have Latin, but it is still worth trying to convey something of the flavour of his language, because it is so intricately bound up with his interpretation of history and his moralising ideology. So, when Tacitus says that the sea was full of exiles (*plenum exiliis mare*), he uses the abstract noun, indicating exile as a concept, rather than the proper noun (*exulibus*), designating exiled people. This linguistic twist should momentarily make us do a double-take, and it has the added advantage of prompting us to dwell on the disturbing phenomenon being described. Tacitus constantly strives after resonant and unusual language, even in quite common words: so, rather than using the standard *omnes* for 'all', he will generally prefer the artificial synonym *cuncti*. Allusive poeticisms and arresting images abound, such as 'cliffs were stained with blood' (*infecti caedibus scopuli*), which recalls descriptions in the epic narratives of the poets Ovid and Statius. Tacitus' gruesome description of the bloody aftermath of perfunctory executions is particularly hard-hitting, because he uses a verb (*infecti*) which has general metaphorical associations with pollution, and chooses a noun in the plural (*caedibus*), where one might have expected a singular form, thereby suggesting slaughter on a grand scale. Finally, Tacitus ends the chapter with a typically paradoxical and hard-hitting *sententia* ('those without an enemy were ruined by their friends'), economically relayed in six words in Latin (*quibus deerat inimicus, per amicos oppressi*) and characterised by a short-circuiting of logic, which deftly encapsulates the moral debasement of the times.

This heady and stimulating 'trailer' has probably already drawn in many hesitant readers in spite of their reservations, but what about the traditionalists, those who were likely to dismiss Tacitus' subject-matter as being deficient in inspiring examples? Tacitus turns to this constituency next, cleverly compartmentalising the previews of disasters, and instead abruptly accentuates the positive, which allows some shafts of light to penetrate the prevailing darkness:

> However, the age was not so utterly barren of virtues that it failed to yield good examples [*bona exempla*] too. Mothers accompanied fleeing sons, wives followed husbands into exile; there were daring kinsmen, devoted sons-in-law, stubbornly loyal slaves, even when tortured; final straits of distinguished men, with the last necessity bravely tolerated and ends matching the laudable deaths of the ancients.
>
> *Histories* 1.3

By such broad categories, Tacitus whets the appetite of his audience for particular uplifting *exempla* and gives a foretaste of how cogently the heroism of individuals can transcend the morally debased era. The use of generalising plurals here is a clever tactic too, since at least some of Tacitus' readers must have been curious about whether their own exploits, or those of prominent members of their family, might in due course be incorporated in the narrative. So, Pliny the Younger, for one, writes to Tacitus an unsolicited letter with details about his own part in a famous case against Baebius Massa in AD 93, in the hopes that it will find a place in the *Histories* and gain lustre as a result (*Letter* 7.33). Even those with more tarnished records may well have anxiously turned to the *Histories* to see whether their own sordid exploits would feature, embarrassingly immortalised to earn the condemnation of generations to come.

The *exempla* which do appear in what survives of the text veer between the laudable and the downright squalid. On the positive side, there is the unnamed Ligurian woman who impressively resists torture by the Othonian soldiers to protect her son (*Histories* 2.13), even if actually we may feel some discomfort at being made voyeurs of such a brutal scene. More depressingly, we witness an eloquently negative *exemplum* in the Flavian soldier who kills his brother, fighting for the other side, and then shockingly demands a reward from his superiors for his 'heroism' (*Histories* 3.51). When the state implodes, family values fly out of the window as well.

Still, what is striking about the notice of *exempla* in the prologue, particularly after the gloomy survey of contents which precedes it, is that Tacitus pointedly shies away from giving advance notice of bad *exempla*, perhaps because that would be to overdo the pessimism. That said, his focus on the deaths of famous men as an enticement to read on may strike a modern audience as being extremely bizarre. After all, what sort of morbid people are these imagined readers to enjoy such a thing?

Yet contemporary audiences certainly seemed to like reading about the deaths of the rich and famous. Seneca the Elder (*c.* 50 BC – AD 40) identifies this as an important and established theme in ancient historiography:

> Whenever the death of some great man has been narrated by historians, almost always an overview of his whole life and, as it were, a funeral laudation are produced. After this was done once or twice by Thucydides, and the technique was likewise used by Sallust for a very few protagonists, Livy generously deployed it for all great men. His successors have used it much more effusively.
>
> *Suasoriae* 6.21

This helpfully pulls the focus back and makes it clear that, even if death-narratives are a pervasive element of Tacitean historiography, they already had an acknowledged place in the genre. Their function was partly to serve as the written counterpart to tributes delivered at funerals, and what initially may seem to us morbid has as much to do with celebration of a great man's life and contribution to society. Indeed, historical narratives were only one forum for such commemorations. We know for example that *exitus* ('death') literature flourished as a genre in its own right: Titinius Capito wrote a work concentrating entirely on the deaths of famous men (Pliny *Letter* 8.12). Besides this, at least in the surviving portion of Tacitus' *Histories*, the narrative is not overwhelmed by extended descriptions of death-scenes (although plenty of people do in fact die). The suicide of the emperor Otho is the one conspicuous instance (*Histories* 2.46-50). Tacitus' moving depiction of his heroic and selfless conduct in his last hours is imbued with subtle touches which recall republican luminaries such as Cato the Younger. These add rich layers to the narrative and problematise the death of someone whose ruthless seizure of power could so easily have indicated a straightforwardly unscrupulous type. Is Otho just an out-and-out villain, who happened to face death bravely, or are there signs that could he have made a decent emperor, if he had not removed himself prematurely by suicide?

Generally today, if people read Tacitus, it tends to be the *Annals* that they turn to first of all. The vibrant portraits of dominating and multifaceted imperial personalities such as Tiberius and Nero, pulling the strings in the oppressive imperial household, or being hoodwinked by wily imperial women, exert a natural fascination. Yet the *Histories* is arguably the more chilling text, in that it graphically and painfully demonstrates what can happen when an imperial structure collapses, and makes clear the price to be paid when the innocent and the vulnerable get caught up in that destruction; and of course, we still have our aggressive imperial powers today, even if such regimes generally try to put a more palatable face on their activities for public consumption.

In the *Histories*, Tacitus constructs a complex narrative of a complex period, imposing meaning on confusing events and artfully juggling multiple spheres of action as pretenders rise (sometimes almost simultaneously at opposite ends of the empire) and emperors fall. What is masterful about this work is that Tacitus not only makes the events themselves accessible, but he also clarifies why they unfolded in the way that they did, avoiding the 'easy' explanations found elsewhere in the parallel tradition. Others who wrote about the civil wars, for example, attributed them simply to the collective madness of the soldiers or put the final victory of Vespasian down to the timely intervention of fortune. Both these ingredients feature in Tacitus' account, but not straightforwardly or in isolation. So, without the subsequent support of the soldiers, Otho would not have been able to retain the principate, but startlingly, it only took a handful of soldiers to make him emperor in the first place (hardly an explosion of collective madness). And Vespasian was indeed lucky enough to win the civil war, but that was more a reflection that his cause happened to attract a talented, charismatic, but morally bankrupt general, Antonius Primus, who circumvented the party's strategy and took matters into his own hands by invading Italy. The alternative 'official' Flavian plan of a cautious advance coupled with a grain blockade of Italy may in the end have got the same results, but the possibility of a population brought to its knees by starvation hardly casts the victors as saints.

The surviving books of the *Histories* offer a kind of 'photo-negative' of traditional Roman historiography, recalling the genre through specific types of scene, but at the same time pointing up the deterioration that has set in between present and past. Thus there are the requisite sweeping battle scenes, but they involve disturbing vistas of Roman fighting Romans in the first (*Histories* 2.39-45) and then the second (*Histories* 3.16-31) battles of Bedriacum in northern Italy. There is a description of a city being sacked, but the place in question is Cremona, a northern Italian town, not some foreign plum ripe for picking (*Histories* 3.33). There are debates in the senate in Rome, broadly evocative of their 'cousins' in republican historiography, but Tacitus' versions tend to reveal the craven and malicious nature of a body, which was once upon a time regarded as exemplifying responsibility and freedom of speech. In one such instance, the influential senator Vibius Priscus prosecutes the malicious Neronian informer Annius Faustus, initially an encouraging development, but it turns out that Priscus himself had profited hugely from being an informer, and the senate emerges as being an institution that is hierarchical, hypocritical and dominated by bullies (*Histories* 2.10-11). Even a miniature ethnographical digression, such as the excursus on the distinctive fighting techniques of the barbarian Sarmatians (*Histories* 1.79), hardly offers straightforward escapism, since it is located in the context of the Roman empire being intensely vulnerable to invasions from such peoples, while its soldiers were concentrating on the business of civil war. These sorts of disturbing inversion of motifs from traditional Roman historiography are naturally most evident in the first three books of the *Histories*, which concentrate on the civil wars, but Tacitus knows how difficult it is for a society to recover from such self-destructive forces. The opening of *Histories* 4 is revealing:

> Vitellius' killing had ended the war more than it had triggered peace. Armed victors throughout the city were hunting down the defeated Vitellians with implacable hatred: the streets were full of killing, the fora and temples were blood-stained, with men slaughtered everywhere, wherever they happened to be found.
>
> *Histories* 4.1

Although the previous book had ended with the death of Vitellius (a traditional closural motif), Tacitus' comment at the start of the next book deliberately creates a jagged and messy opening, which underscores how difficult it will be for the Roman state to draw a real line underneath the civil wars. A military victory is one thing, but terminating the violence and healing the psychological scars is something quite different, and inevitably much more prolonged. It feels as if we are entering a twilight zone, with the morality and problems of the civil wars still overflowing uncontrollably into the present and choking Roman efforts to recover.

Symptomatic of this process is another bastardised element of the narrative, evocative of traditional historiography, but different, namely an (apparently) foreign war which dominates *Histories* 4 and 5. In previous historians such as Livy, the calibre of foreign leaders challenges and brings out the best in the Roman protagonists, forcing them to draw deeply on their reserves of energy and bravery. Livy's dynamic Carthaginian general Hannibal is perhaps the best example of a challenging enemy, who makes the Romans excel by stretching their resources to the limit. When Tacitus first introduces Julius Civilis, the energetic and colourful one-eyed leader of a barbarian rebellion involving German tribes (*Histories* 4.12-37, 4.54-79, 5.14-26), it looks for a moment as if we are reverting to a more comforting historiographical mode, dominated by familiar polarities between Rome and the enemy. Here at last is a foreign foe, an antidote to all of the disastrous self-destruction of the first three books. Yet it turns out that Julius Civilis is in fact a devious Roman auxiliary leader (and so not a true outsider at all), who merely adopts the guise of a barbarian leader and calls the tribes to fight for their freedom, after in fact being invited to stir up diversionary trouble by the Flavian general

2. *The Peak of Creativity*

Antonius Primus (*Histories* 4.13). What sort of war is this then? It is not straightforwardly a continuation of the civil war, since it certainly involves foreign elements on the front-line, who genuinely believe that they are fighting for independence from Rome. Yet at the same time, it has evolved as a direct result from Roman activities in the civil war, now notionally finished. Tacitus draws attention to its slippery, messy identity by calling it a 'mixed' conflict (*Histories* 1.2) and 'simultaneously civil and foreign' (*Histories* 2.69).

According to a well-established tenet of the republic, what would really benefit Rome at this point is a good dose of *metus hostilis*, 'fear of the enemy', that is the beneficial and unifying terror of the outsider, which makes citizens bury their petty internal differences, stop questioning their leaders, and pull together for the greater good of the state. It is a phenomenon which has extended the political life of many a modern leader, whether we think of Margaret Thatcher's landslide election victory in 1983, after winning the Falklands war in the previous year, or George Bush's triumph over his opponent John Kerry in 2004, after Osama bin Laden issued a timely taped diatribe against him a few days before the Americans cast their votes. Yet the war against Julius Civilis will not straightforwardly fulfil the requirements of *metus hostilis* to aid the process of recovery within the Roman state. This only begins to happen when Tacitus turns his attention to the Jews (with whom Vespasian has been engaged in a war on behalf of the Roman state since before the civil wars started and now being run by his son Titus). In an (infamous) ethnographical excursus on the Jews (*Histories* 5.2-13), Tacitus outlines their history, customs and religious practices in terms of the 'other'. Jewish culture is presented as an inversion of everything that a Roman reader would regard as normal, and the tone is, at best, perplexed, and at worst, hostile. Jewish exclusivity, monotheism, burial practices and so forth are described for Roman consumption in language that is starkly polarising and often pejorative.

This section of the *Histories*, perhaps more than any other, tends to make modern readers uneasy, and the hostile excursus has certainly been mined in the past for material to serve as anti-semitic propaganda, just as the *Germania* was appropriated to endorse Nazi ideology. We need, however, to understand the context of Tacitus' formal ethnographical excursus on the Jews before we throw up our hands in despair. For it plays a crucial transitional part in extricating the historical narrative from the self-destructive ethos of the civil wars. It is a section in which the Roman state makes the leap from self-destructive civil wars to a foreign campaign. Now domestic and external national identities are once again contrasted and the differences between opposing sides are (finally) more prominent than the disturbing similarities that had characterised the protagonists of those successive conflicts in which Roman fought Roman. This 'restorative' function of the excursus is, however, masked by the fact that the *Histories* breaks off at 5.26, leaving so much of the Jewish war still to be narrated. In fact, the striking point about *Histories* 4-5 is not that Tacitus devoted so much attention to the Jews, but that he treated the Batavian revolt (almost ignored by our other sources) so extensively. The more reassuring character of the Jewish war (signalled forcefully by the formal ethnographical excursus) is in sharp contrast with the much more murky world exemplified by the shifting identities of Julius Civilis and his Batavians.

The extraordinary dominance of Tacitus in allowing modern

historians access to the principate becomes especially clear when we consider the frustratingly inadequate evidence that exists in comparison for those periods when his narrative is lost. If his account of the Flavians in the *Histories* had survived, then no doubt modern studies of this period would be as ebullient, stimulating and prolific as they are for the Julio-Claudian era. Alternative narratives such as Suetonius' biographies are engaging in their own right (and to be fair, they have a different agenda), but they do not provide the sort of sophisticated chronological or interpretative framework which makes reading Tacitus so absorbing. The problem is exacerbated by the phenomenon in the ancient world whereby a successful historian's work tended to supersede his predecessors' accounts of the same period. If a historian did well, then alternative versions would be eclipsed. Pliny the Younger, for one, is supremely confident that Tacitus' historical narrative will supersede any others (an endorsement which implicitly testifies to the enthusiastic reception of the 'minor works'):

> I predict, and the augury does not deceive me, that your histories will be immortal.
>
> *Letter* 7.33

If only Pliny had been right about the vagaries of manuscript survival as well as the about the calibre of Tacitus' historiography – but it was not to be.

... Decline: The Annals

After the *Histories*, Tacitus could have written about any number of different periods, but he chose to focus on the four

Julio-Claudian emperors, Tiberius (AD 14-37), Caligula (AD 37-41), Claudius (AD 41-54) and Nero (AD 54-68), conspicuously omitting Augustus (31 BC – AD 14), the tricky architect of the imperial system, except in flashbacks. But the *Annals*, like the *Histories*, has suffered the loss of significant portions: most of book 5, some of book 6, and all of books 7-10 are gone, while book 16 breaks off at chapter 35, which means that portions of Tiberius', Claudius' and Nero's principates are missing, as well as the whole of Caligula's. After Tacitus' assertion that he was 'saving' the principates of Nerva and Trajan for his old age (*Histories* 1.1), some have seen his retrospection and avoidance of that material as reflecting disillusion with the current emperor. We need not read it this way, however. After all, when Tacitus started the *Annals*, he did not know that it was going to be his last work, so the projected history of Nerva and Trajan was still a possibility. In any case, from the standpoint of AD 109 (the publication date of the *Histories*), after having already covered Domitian, he may have considered that not enough material had yet accrued from the principates of Nerva and Trajan to flesh out a historical narrative. In any case, it was likely that such a project would be much better served by waiting until Trajan was dead. There was certainly a risk that Tacitus' credibility would be perceived as compromised (whatever the reality), if he chose to write about a living emperor. Pliny the Elder chose to postpone the publication of his historical work, *A History of Our Times*, until after he was dead, so that people would not think of it as a self-serving vehicle (*Natural History*, preface 20). And it is conspicuous that Velleius Paterculus, one of the few historians between Livy and Tacitus whose work has survived, for a long time met with a dismissive reception from modern scholars because he wrote enthusiastically about Tiberius, the emperor under whom he lived. Tacitus' career would continue to flourish under Trajan, culminating in the prestigious proconsulship of Asia (AD 112-13). For him to write about someone whose patronage he was actively enjoying would be pointless. He was not the sort of man to serve as a court-historian, as Aristotle's nephew Callisthenes did for Alexander the Great.

Besides, there were also cogent intellectual reasons for pushing his focus back to examine the period that led up to the civil wars of AD 68-9 and the new Flavian dynasty that followed. Even within a single work, historians in the ancient world often laid down preparatory analysis of the period running up to their chosen subject to enhance understanding and establish causal links. So, although the Greek historian Thucydides' main topic was the Peloponnesian war (431-404 BC), he devoted his first book to exploring the background to the conflict, including the *Pentecontaetia* (*Peloponnesian War* 1.89-118), which considered the events between 479 and 435 BC, which helped to explain why Athens was so strong at the start of the war. Similarly, Polybius, whose central topic was the extraordinary rise to prominence of Roman power between 220 and 168 BC, devotes his first two books to exploring the background from 264 BC onwards, to allow his readers to orientate themselves. He justifies himself as follows:

One must take up a starting-point appropriate to the circumstances, which is recognisable by everyone and which can be seen clearly from events, even though it may necessitate retracing one's steps briefly to summarise the intervening affairs. For if the starting-point is unknown or, by Zeus, in dispute, nothing of what follows can win approval or credibility. Once a consensus has been reached about this, then the whole of the following argument wins acceptance from the audience.

Histories 1.5

We can see how the starting-point of a historical narrative was always difficult for an author to pin down. Many historians felt obliged, for the sake of their readers, to explain later events by pushing the focus back to clarify the root causes, which emerged before the formal beginning of the narrative proper. Tacitus, while writing the *Histories*, perhaps concluded on this basis that a 'prequel' would be highly desirable, both to lay down in greater detail why the civil wars of AD 68-9 erupted and to explore the structures of the earlier principate that the Flavians, each in different ways, were remodelling. The result was a dove-tailed progression of two narratives, which future readers could follow in chronological sequence, with Julio-Claudian decline in the *Annals* preceding fall (and Flavian reconstruction) in the *Histories*, despite the order in which Tacitus had originally written them. That potential reorganisation is reflected in the fact that a later editor combined the two works in precisely this way, for Jerome (*c.* AD 347-420) refers to thirty books of (what he calls) Tacitus' *Lives of the Caesars*, which means that he was reading a consolidated edition. Tacitus' perception of the advantages in such an inter-connected pairing of narratives is perhaps also indicated by his claim that subsequently, he intends to go even further back in time to write about the period before Tiberius' accession

(*Annals* 3.24). How seriously we should take such pledges is unclear. Historians often made them, and Lucian parodies the tendency at the end of his *True Histories* (a fantastic adventure narrative which includes a trip to the moon) with his mock-serious promise: 'What happened on the continent I shall relate in books to follow' (*True Histories* 2.47). Needless to say, Lucian never wrote such a work.

Although in the *Annals*, Tacitus goes further back in time, he still faces some of the same challenges that he confronted in the *Histories* from his choice of subject-matter. In a digression comparing the material of his own history with those writing narratives about distant history, he says:

> … many who suffered punishment or disgrace under Tiberius' principate have living descendants, and, even if the families themselves have now been extinguished, you will discover people who think that they are being charged through the misdeeds of others because of their similar behaviour. Even glory and courage provoke hostility, since they are too close for comfort in blaming the opposite traits.
>
> *Annals* 4.33

Tacitus may complain here about the sensitivities of his contemporary audience, some of whom see criticism of themselves in his denunciations of figures from the past, but he is being disingenuous. In practice, such hints of similarities and shared characteristics, which collapse the chronological gulf between different eras, are very useful to him. It all helps to create an atmosphere of *déjà vu*, which he triggers provocatively, even at the very opening of the narrative:

81

> The city of Rome from the beginning was held by kings [*urbem Romam a principio reges habuere*].
>
> *Annals* 1.1

This is indeed an artful beginning, rich in ambiguity and double-meaning, and implicitly posing an inflammatory question. Since Tacitus pointedly says that Rome was held by kings, not 'in the beginning', but 'from the beginning', we wonder about the nature of the comparison being posited with the present. In the past, Rome was held by kings – but unlike it is now under the principate? Or just as it is today under the principate? Is even Trajan is some sense a king? Tacitus defuses the tension temporarily by the next juxtaposed clause, before which we have to supply a 'but': 'Lucius Brutus established freedom and the consulship' (*Annals* 1.1). Yet even this addition is ambiguous. Tacitus' primary reference is to the Brutus who expelled the last of the kings, Tarquinius Superbus, and liberated the state by instituting the republic in 509 BC, but we may also think here of this man's descendant, the Brutus who re-enacted that liberation by taking a leading role in Caesar's assassination in 44 BC. Although we may initially think we are getting some sort of diachronic survey of the evolution of the Roman state at the start of the *Annals*, Tacitus actually seems to be asking how much has really changed over the centuries. This becomes even clearer if we consider that his opening sentence alludes to the preface of Sallust's *Catiline*, specifically to his retrospective survey of the development of Rome:

> The city of Rome, as I have heard, was founded and held in the beginning by Trojans [*Vrbem Romam, sicuti ego accepi, condidere atque habuere initio Troiani*].
>
> *Catiline* 6

2. The Peak of Creativity

Sallust unambiguously has 'in the beginning', rather than 'from the beginning', and he acknowledges the Trojans as Rome's founders, a point (and a period in the city's history) glossed over by Tacitus, who immediately and suggestively zooms in on the kings. The contrast with Sallust helps to bring out more clearly how provocative Tacitus is being in his opening sentence. Modern historians might bring in similar comparisons in their own narratives, but no doubt they would achieve this by an explicit footnote in their text, pointing readers in the direction of the relevant parallel. Tacitus embeds such points in the very language which he uses. It is one of the reasons why reading his narratives is so engaging. He does not always make it easy for us, but if we read with a critical eye, the layers are there to be teased apart.

This sort of meaningful historical underpinning continues in the narrative itself. So when Tacitus narrates the death of Augustus, he points out how Augustus' wife (or widow, actually) Livia cordoned off the house and continued to post encouraging news about her husband's state of health, even though he was in fact dead (*Annals* 1.5). Her reason for doing this (Tacitus implies) was that she wanted to wait until her son Tiberius (Augustus' step-son) was on the scene before informing people that her husband was dead, thus aiding her son's accession. The way in which Tacitus describes events artfully recalls a well-known sequence from the regal period, told in detail by Livy (*From the Foundation of the City* 1.41). The fifth king of Rome, Tarquinius Priscus, an immigrant, took power after the death of his predecessor, Ancus Marcius, despite the fact that this man had sons of his own. These displaced heirs eventually attacked Priscus, hoping to regain power. When the king lay dying, his enterprising wife Tanaquil promptly closed the palace and announced to the people that her husband would soon recover, but she suggested that in the meantime, they should obey her son (and Tarquinius' son-in-law), Servius Tullius. The illusion that Priscus was still alive was maintained for a few days, by which point the succession of Servius was guaranteed. Tacitus deliberately narrates the succession of Tiberius so as to map the regal family onto their imperial counterparts: Augustus is Tarquinius Priscus, Livia plays the Tanaquil character, and Tiberius becomes Servius Tullius. Even the fact that Augustus has an exiled grandson of his own, Agrippa Postumus, with whom he allegedly made up shortly before his death, coheres with the Livian intertext with its focus on the displaced rivals for power, the sons of Ancus Marcius. So dynastic power struggles mark both narratives and bind them together.

What are we to make of this? Evoking the regal period so vividly at Tiberius' succession is an extraordinary move. Some modern critics see such touches as adding rhetorical colour, rather than offering a valid tool for historical interpretation, but we can challenge this view. After all, Augustus himself was at pains to dissociate his new role in the state from the regal period, as we can see from his swift rejection of the honorific title Romulus, the name of the first king, suggested by some senators (Suetonius *Augustus* 7). Tacitus' echoes of the events surrounding Tarquinius Priscus' death also cohere with his striking decision to begin his historical narrative with Tiberius, not Augustus. For with the accession of Tiberius, people finally had to stop deluding themselves that the system of government developed by Augustus was anything other than autocratic and hereditary. At this very moment of unmasking the realities of

2. The Peak of Creativity

power in AD 14, Tacitus summons up of the regal period to raise central questions, which go right to the heart of the evolving nature of the principate.

In his historical works, Tacitus consistently uses the past to set up a meaningful dialogue with the present (both the 'now' internal to his narrative and the external 'now' of his own era). Decoding the allusions or opening them up for debate would of course rest on the ingenuity and engagement of the audience, and Tacitus certainly assumes a sophisticated readership, tuned in to its own history and familiar with the works of its eminent practitioners. It is worth remembering in this context that exposure to texts in the ancient world was very often a sociable, collective activity: reading in isolation certainly happened, but authors would set up readings of their works (and works-in-progress) before invited audiences, who would no doubt discuss the texts with each other after the readings. The young emperor Claudius, for instance, gave a public reading of a Roman history which he was writing, but was forced to stop when he repeatedly dissolved in giggles after a fat man came in and broke the bench on which he had tried to sit down (Suetonius *Claudius* 41). In normal circumstances, the public context of such readings would mean that the significance of any allusions in a text would serve as fodder for lively discussions. No doubt one such talking point would have been Tacitus' introductory description of the emperor Tiberius' notorious and power-hungry right-hand man, Sejanus, who became increasingly dominant in controlling access to the emperor, until his abrupt downfall in AD 30:

His body was tolerant of labours, his mind was bold. Cagey on his own behalf, he made charges against others. Fawning and

Tacitus

arrogance went hand in hand. On the surface, he wore a mask of modesty, but within, there was a desire for acquiring supremacy, and for that reason there was sometimes extravagance and luxuriousness, but more often industry and vigilance – no less harmful when they are fashioned towards procuring power.

Annals 4.1

A figure combining such strength and intellectual acuity with just the wrong kind of personal ambition is clearly always going to be dangerous. In addition to the alarm-bells triggered by the description, it is conspicuous that Tacitus has postponed Sejanus' introduction to the start of book four to signal his importance, even though he could have featured earlier in the narrative. Already then his audience would have their ears pricked. However, what would be especially striking about this character-sketch is the extensive echoing of a well-known passage from Sallust, describing the notorious republican politician (and subject of the monograph), Catiline, who organised a conspiracy in 63 BC. The nature of the plot is controversial, but thanks largely to Cicero, Catiline became the archetype of the 'public enemy' and was defeated and killed in battle in 62 BC. Sallust describes him as follows:

His body was tolerant of hunger, cold, vigilance, more than is credible for any man. His mind, bold, crafty, and versatile, was capable of any pretence and dissimulation; coveting what belonged to others, he was extravagant with his own resources and burned in pursuing his passions. Although quite an eloquent man, he lacked wisdom. His insatiable ambition was always lusting after the extravagant, impossible and unattainable. After the dictatorship of Sulla, the greatest lust for seizing the state had taken hold of this man. He did not care how he achieved this as long as he got power for himself.

Catiline 5

Through a series of linguistic echoes and structural similarities to this passage in the Latin, Tacitus suggests a parallelism between two thoroughly dangerous individuals. Catiline and Sejanus may have been operating in different political systems and are separated by almost a hundred years, but the implication is that they were the same kind of creatures, mentally and physically gifted, but ruthlessly capable. Tacitus could have made a similar point simply by explicitly saying that Sejanus was 'just like Catiline', but the imprint of ghostly footprints in his text is much more subtle. There is an analogy perhaps in George Clooney's film, *Good Night and Good Luck*, about the broadcaster Ed Murrow's response to McCarthy and the House Committee on un-American Activities in the 1950s, which was able to create a climate of fear, partly because of collective paralysis in some sections of the media, who offered an insufficiently robust response to McCarthy's activities. The film makes implicit comparisons with the contemporary scene, and with growing concerns that the American media has been inadequate in challenging the US government's dubious disregard for civil liberties in the name of a war on terror. The parallels are allowed to emerge suggestively through the renewed relevance of Murrow's powerful rhetoric, and we see that ghostly footprints can still be a highly expressive device.

That unsettling sense of having seen something before is also evident within individual sections of Tacitus' narrative, sometimes widely separated. Thus he opens his account of Tiberius' principate with a reference to 'the first crime of the new regime' [*primum facinus noui principatus*] (*Annals* 1.6). This is sufficiently pejorative in its own right, but it becomes even more laden with meaning when we reach Nero's principate. As Ronald Martin has pointed out, Tacitus' opening salvo against Nero is highly evocative of the earlier Tiberian passage: 'the first death in the new regime' [*prima novo principatu mors*] (*Annals* 13.1). We are left with the unavoidable feeling that although the personnel may have changed, the corrupt imperial system lurches along in the same old way.

In a passage which has already come up in discussion, the digression about the subject-matter of the *Annals*, Tacitus memorably implies that his own material is utterly trivial and depressing compared with 'proper' historical narratives:

> I am well aware that most of what I have recorded, and will record, perhaps seems slight and trivial to recall; but nobody should compare my annals with the writing of those who compiled the history of the ancient Roman people. They had free rein to narrate huge wars, cities being stormed, routed and captured kings, or, whenever they turned their attention to internal affairs, disputes between consuls and tribunes, agrarian and grain laws, and contests of *plebs* and *optimates*. Yet my work is trammelled and ignoble: peace was unbroken or only moderately disturbed, matters in the city were sorrowful, and the *princeps* lacked interest in extending the empire.
>
> *Annals* 4.32

Yet the positioning of this authorial outburst, well into Tacitus' first hexad (group of six books), is actually rather mischievous. If a reader has got this far through the narrative, then that implies some considerable engagement with the text, and even enjoyment of it. The concession at this point that this narrative is not good old republican history prompts readers to pause and consider their motives for reading on: entering Tacitus' world is not straightforwardly pleasurable, but it does have a certain compulsion and fascination to it, as the audience becomes steeped in the guilty pleasures of watching a disaster narrative unfold. For Roman readers, that heady combination of guilt and pleasure would be especially powerful, because it is *their* state, *their* ancestors and *their* city which are the focus. The dynamic of Tacitus' digression is rather as if the grim-faced anchor person, co-ordinating the rolling news coverage of the latest terrorist attacks, were to step out of character for a moment to ask the viewers (or voyeurs) 'You all know what has happened. Why are you watching this?', yet still confident that the audience will nevertheless resume its viewing after the troubling question has been posed. What Tacitus' readers see when the narrative resumes will be the historian Cremutius Cordus, hauled before the senate for making positive references to Brutus and Cassius in his writings, and then committing suicide. Cremutius Cordus' attempts to dismiss the relevance of his comments on the grounds that it all happened a long time ago, and that his writing is hardly going to inflame the people and stir up civil war, are in fact subtly undercut by Tacitus' preceding digression. If Tacitus' readers have reflected thoughtfully on their motives for continuing to read this apparently 'unstimulating' account of Tiberius' principate, then the notion that historical texts *are* powerful entities will have just been brought home to them with a bump, and Cordus' words will ring hollow. That does not of course justify burning his books, but it does underscore the huge emotional power of historiography.

In the *Annals*, there are numerous examples of intensely vivid scenes, which are simultaneously shocking, yet compulsive and enjoyable in a warped way, offering Tacitus' readers what we might call *gaudium crudele* ('cruel delight'). This is phrase used by the poet Martial to describe the song of the mythical Sirens, which was impossible to refrain from hearing, however much one wanted to blot it out (Martial *Epigrams* 3.64.2). Tacitus has a similar oxymoron (*misera laetitia*, 'melancholy delight' *Histories* 2.45) to describe the victors and vanquished contemplating the civil war after the first battle of Bedriacum, but it could apply equally well to the whole experience of reading his historical narratives. A particularly extreme instance is the description of a banquet organised by Nero's praetorian prefect, Tigellinus, which Tacitus says that he is narrating an 'example' (*exemplum*) to prevent him having to relate such scenes too often. That term *exemplum* activates the moralising dimension of historiography at a particularly apt point:

So, on the lake of Agrippa, Tigellinus built a pontoon, on which a party was set up and moved along by the towing of other ships. The ships were decorated with gold and ivory; and the rowers, male prostitutes, were arranged by age and expertise in lust. He had sought birds and wild beasts from all manner of lands, and animals of the sea all the way from the Ocean. On the banks of the pool stood brothels filled with illustrious ladies, and opposite, whores were on view with their naked bodies. Already there were obscene gestures and movements; but after darkness began to fall, every nearby copse and the surrounding houses rang out with singing and gleamed with lights. Nero himself, defiled by acts permitted and illicit, had left no perversion untried in his effort to become more corrupt, except that after a few days, he took one of that gang of perverts (his name was Pythagoras) as his husband in a solemn wedding ceremony. The marriage veil was placed on the emperor [*imperatori*], the officials were sent for; dowry, marriage-bed, wedding torches …. In short, everything was observed, which even in a real woman, the night covers up.

Annals 15.37

Tacitus pulls out all the stops in this dazzling passage to hammer home the utter degradation and squalor now emanating from the emperor Nero and his hedonistic entourage. The party is an expressive distillation of the corrupted and corrupting spirit of a morally blind man: Nero does not remotely care if his kaleidoscopic decadence is on display, caught up as he is in a craven world which collaborates so enthusiastically and obligingly with all his whims. Indeed, by the prevailing internal logic of Neronian Rome, the emperor is not actually doing anything wrong. Yet in the outer frame, inhabited by Tacitus and his audience, every detail becomes nauseating and repellent. The party takes place on the lake of Agrippa, that is Augustus' general, whose hard work helped to win the very same empire, whose rich resources are now being so lavishly frittered away. The focus on all those exotic creatures, which had been shipped in from the imperial margins, graphically demonstrates how Rome's economically privileged position at the centre of the world, the *orbis terrarum*, is being abused, as luxury goods are imported to indulge the fancies of the decadent. Tacitus' list of birds, wild beasts and animals is a rhetorical device called *enumeratio*, which makes the 'whole' more graphic by listing its parts, and it is powerfully redeployed at the end of the passage in the catalogue of Nero's dowry, marriage-bed and wedding torches. All of this is enhanced by Tacitus conspicuously focusing at different points on the visual dimension ('whores were on view; gleamed with lights; everything was observed'). Well-written historical accounts ideally used techniques of *enargeia*, 'vividness', to enable readers to enter the world of the narrative by visualising particular scenes, and piling up of words associated with seeing was one component of this trope. Tacitus certainly does that here, but to any Roman with moral backbone, it would have felt like stepping into a landscape of nightmare.

Another disturbing element of the passage (at least to Roman elite eyes) is the elision of distinctions between the highest and lowest rungs of the social hierarchy. There is a mocking evocation of the proper divisions, when Tacitus locates the 'illustrious ladies' on one side of the pool and the 'prostitutes' on the other side, but both groups are now fused together by their shared sexual activities. A related point is the gender-bending, particularly from Nero in the finale of the passage. The emperor's fake marriage inevitably crops up in other sources, including Suetonius (*Nero* 28), but Tacitus' version has a special twist. For (unlike Suetonius) he describes the ceremony with the Latin verb, *denubo*, which applies specifically when a woman marries a man, and thus casts Nero in the female role. That is coupled with the pointed use of the term *imperator* for Nero, evoking not just his role as emperor, but the military responsibilities of the office. Tacitus does this at just the point when Nero's behaviour most vividly shows his utter derision for the position. Nero's capacity for boundary-breaking is anticipated when Tacitus appears to draw a firm line around the emperor's comprehensive delinquency, only to move the goalposts with the addition of the sequence about the marriage ('Nero had left no perversion untried in his effort to become more corrupt, *except* …'). Just when you think that it can't get any worse, it does: in the perversely inventive world of Tacitus' narrative, superlatives or absolute categories are constantly vulnerable to being superseded and overshadowed by something even more extreme.

Tacitus lets this passage speak for itself, allowing the moralism to emerge from his description, rather than indulging in a thundering and extended denunciation of Nero's conduct. Even so, there is more than a hint of retribution in the way that Tacitus begins the next chapter (*Annals* 15.38), which is another purple passage about the great fire of Rome in AD 64. All he says is: 'Disaster followed.' The juxtaposition of the party-scene and the fire is hugely powerful, particularly since Tacitus could have included the representative revelry more or less anywhere he wanted in his narrative. Yet it comes here, with the corrupt 'wedding torches' serving as an elegant transitional device to the famous fire in the city. The arrangement of the narrative implies that the outbreak and progress of this apocalyptic conflagration, however it started, is potentially something of a catharsis for Rome. The fire seems to be an utterly destructive, but cleansing force, with the potential to get rid of all this detritus. In the end, however, even something that deadly cannot stop the rot, as Nero takes advantage of the new space created in Rome to build his Golden House, promptly re-imposing his corrupting influence on the city.

Blistering passages like these have left some readers of Tacitus distinctly uneasy that they are being manipulated. The French historian Voltaire, for instance, who once said that 'History is after all nothing but a parcel of tricks that we play on the dead', was concerned that Tacitus was dealing in fiction, rather than fact, and speculated that his techniques were symptomatic of 'a malicious wit, who poisons everything through the medium of a concise and energetic style'. It is certainly true that if we use the yardstick of modern historical enquiry to measure Tacitus' *Histories* and *Annals*, they will often be found wanting. Yet, as Joseph Mitchell once wrote: 'In autobiography and biography, as in history, I have discovered there are occasions when the facts do not tell the truth' (*Joe Gould's Secret*, 1965). Establishing 'what really happened' was not the most urgent priority for Tacitus. By the standards of his own time, Tacitus was using his creative powers of imagination to shape brilliant narratives, which would in turn give something back to his own age by reminding contemporaries how low it was possible for their state to sink and prompting them to foster their own integrity and independence at every opportunity. A powerful indication of Tacitus' continuing relevance lies in the fact that, since the eighteenth century, there have been several attempts to prove that his works were forged. The most conspicuous was when the texts took on a new lease of life during the French revolution, when Tacitus' perceived republicanism proved an inspiration: the emperor Napoleon made serious efforts to discredit the works as fakes. That is eloquent proof indeed of Tacitus' powerful historiographical voice.

3

From Hellraisers to Heroes:
The Afterlife of Julius Civilis and Arminius

Introduction

The 'afterlife' of Tacitus' historical narratives, rich and lively though it is, hangs precariously by thin threads, since only two manuscripts saved them from total oblivion and loss. The story of their preservation is worth telling. The first manuscript, containing the text of *Annals* 1-6, was written in Germany (perhaps in the Benedictine abbey of Fulda) in the middle of the ninth century and now preserved in the Biblioteca Laurenziana in Florence. This is the library of the Medici prince, Lorenzo the Magnificent, so the manuscript is called the *codex Mediceus*, or just M for short. For centuries it sat neglected in the monastery of Corvey in Saxony without being copied, but in 1508 it was removed from the library, apparently at the bidding of Pope Leo X, who had paid a large sum of money for it. The 'hunt' for this particular manuscript had certainly been going on for some time and Leo was not the first to try to get hold of it. After his coup in securing M, Pope Leo passed it to Filippo Beraldo the Younger, who produced the first edition of Tacitus' *Annals* in 1515.

The second (later) manuscript, containing *Annals* 11-16 and *Histories* 1-5, was written in Beneventan script at Monte Cassino in the eleventh century and is now called M II, the 'second Medicean'. As we will see, it was generally 'better-trav-elled' than the first manuscript, M, and indeed, the fact that people knew about it seems ultimately to have generated interest in M, which had been sitting for all that time in the monastery of Corvey in Saxony. Even M II had kept a reasonably low profile in the monastery at Monte Cassino for several centuries, but by 1371, Giovanni Boccaccio had seen the manuscript and acquired it. At his death, he gave it to the monastery of San Spirito in Florence. It next appears in 1427 in the hands of Niccolo Niccoli, who had made bookcases for Boccaccio's collection at the monastery. He appears to have acquired it in distinctly suspicious circumstances. For his friend Poggio Bracciolini, desperate to see the text, wrote to him as follows:

> Now to more important matters. When the Cornelius Tacitus comes, I shall keep it hidden with me, for I know that whole song 'Where did it come from and who brought it here? Who claims it for his own?'. But do not worry, not a word shall escape me …. I have heard nothing about the Cornelius Tacitus which is in Germany. I am waiting for an answer from that monk …. Rome, the twenty-fifth of September, 1427.
>
> Bracciolini *Letter* 51

When Niccoli himself died in 1437, the manuscript passed to the monastery of San Marco in Florence, and copies finally began to be made. From San Marco, the manuscript was trans-ferred (at some date) to the Biblioteca Laurenziana in Florence. A crucial stage was the production of the first printed edition of *Histories* 1-5 and *Annals* 11-16 by the press of 'Spira' in Venice (undated, but generally assumed to be from 1468 or 1470). Yet it was not until the first printed edition of 1515 that these later books of the *Annals* were 'reunited' with *Annals* 1-6 by Beraldo.

The history of manuscripts can certainly be a fascinating subject in its own right. Indeed, another *codex* now in the Biblioteca Nazionale in Rome and which preserved Tacitus' minor works (including the *Germania*) even attracted the attention of Adolf Hitler, who asked Mussolini for the manuscript. It was not in the event handed over, despite Mussolini's initial agreement, and in 1944 SS troops were sent to Italy to search for the manuscript, which eluded their attention, since it was hidden in a kitchen cellar in a wooden trunk. It sounds extraordinary that such efforts were made to acquire this *codex* during a war, but manuscripts naturally became valuable treasures in their own right, particularly if they contained a text like the *Germania*, which had important contemporary resonances. Moreover, not all owners cared for the contents of these manuscripts, which could serve as an invaluable way to keep their money safe in a financially unstable world. They had the advantage of being uniquely valuable and highly portable (especially compared with alternatives such as gold).

At any rate, the enthusiastic hunt for manuscripts carried out by men such as Poggio Bracciolini and sponsored by the Popes, who were eager to stock the Vatican library with works from antiquity, meant that the manuscripts of Tacitus were in the public eye once more, after centuries of neglect. With the discovery of printing, the texts were exposed to an even wider audience after the first printed editions began to appear and circulate in the late fifteenth and early sixteenth centuries. In this final chapter, we will follow the (related) stories of two significant figures from Tacitus' historical narratives, the

3. From Hellraisers to Heroes

Batavian rebel leader Julius Civilis from the *Histories* and the Cheruscan troublemaker Arminius from the *Annals*. Both Civilis and Arminius were historical figures, but it was above all Tacitus who put flesh on their bones and 'created' protagonists, who would now take on a life of their own, after all those years in the twilight.

Julius Civilis and the Dutch

The intriguing figure of Julius Civilis has already come up several times in our discussion so far. This former Roman auxiliary leader, scornfully dubbed by the Vitellian soldiers a 'Batavian turncoat' (*Histories* 4.21), seems to have exerted a strange fascination on Tacitus, who took the trouble to relay a very detailed narrative of the whole Batavian revolt (*Histories* 4.12-37, 4.54-79, 5.14-26), even though our other sources for the period virtually ignore it. Yet, as we will see, where Tacitus originally characterised Julius Civilis as a devious leader of a grubby, murky and opportunistic revolt, Dutch writers and artists in the fifteenth and sixteenth centuries eagerly seized upon him to create something very different, triggering his remarkable metamorphosis into an emotive symbol of freedom and national identity. In the prevailing political climate, they urgently needed to find a hero, and Tacitus' Julius Civilis, endorsed by the stamp of antiquity, fitted the bill beautifully. If they had to reshape him to some extent to wash off some of the dirt, then so be it.

Before we consider that transformation, however, it is useful to remind ourselves about the broad character of Julius Civilis in Tacitus' original text. Both the timing and the location of his revolt, with the powerful German tribes so close and the Roman forces not yet back to full operational levels after the civil wars, meant that it had the potential to be extremely dangerous. Tacitus' Civilis, whose very name is so suggestive of a civil conflict, is characterised as a clever chameleon, who can play up his barbarian or Roman identity depending on the circumstances:

> Yet Civilis had a more versatile mind than barbarians usually do, and declared himself to be another Sertorius or Hannibal because of a similar facial disfigurement [*simili oris dehonestamento*], although he made a pretence of friendship with Vespasian and enthusiasm for the cause, fearing that if he openly rebelled against the Roman people, an attack might be made on him as an enemy...
>
> *Histories* 4.13

Roman authors traditionally cast northern barbarians as rather slow-witted clodhoppers, whose poor brains were frozen into stupidity by the bitterly cold climate in which they lived, so Tacitus needs to counteract this preconception by casting Civilis as unusually intelligent. He must have cut quite a figure: with his wounded face and empty eye-socket, Civilis was unmistakable to onlookers. In fact, he probably lost his eye while fighting for Rome as an auxiliary leader, so his exploitation of the wound in the persona of a romantic rebel is especially audacious. And the two famous one-eyed figures from Roman history conjured up by Civilis are deftly chosen to enhance his stature. The Carthaginian leader Hannibal came as close as anyone to bringing down the Roman state, particularly at the battle of Cannae in 216 BC, where he defeated both consuls and their armies; and the rebel Roman general Sertorius led a concerted resistance against the dictator Sulla in Spain, gaining widespread support by adopting native clothing and speaking the local language (Plutarch *Sertorius* 3). In an elegant touch, Tacitus reinforces Civilis' practical evocation of Sertorius with a literary allusion to a surviving fragment about Sertorius from the *Histories* of Sallust (rather in the way that he used allusion to cast Sejanus as a second Catiline). Sallust refers to Sertorius' gouged-out eye and battle-scars collectively as 'disfigurement of his body' (*dehonestamentum corporis, Histories* 1.88), and Tacitus uses the same choice Latin word (*simili oris dehonestamento*) to refer the one-eyed Civilis, which brilliantly makes his Civilis and Sallust's Sertorius coalesce, despite the chronological gap between the pair. This strident and evocative self-presentation, however, sits very oddly with Civilis' soothing assertion of friendship with Vespasian. In the opening character-sketch, Tacitus quickly establishes Civilis' dangerously slippery and shifting identity.

Nor is it just Civilis who has chameleon characteristics – his Batavian troops seem to be playing the same sort of game. They have, after all, seen long service under the Romans, and as Art Pomeroy has said, their liminal status colours their depiction throughout the *Histories*. One trait that Tacitus identifies at an early stage is their ability to swim across the Rhine with ease (*Histories* 4.12), which is certainly an appropriate skill for metaphorical boundary-crossers such as these. Their duplicity comes out in an early military clash by the Rhine:

Batavians made up some of the rowers and, faking incompetence, they began to hamper the sailors and marines in carrying

out their duties, but then they actively struggled against them
and steered the boats towards the enemy's bank ...

Histories 4.16

If the Batavians had simply switched sides before the conflict
started, then they would have done much less damage, but there
is something curious about the nature of their *volte-face*. By
feigning clumsiness, the Batavian rowers are themselves playing
the role of barbarians as constructed by Greek and Roman ethnographical writers. Ungainliness is a trait frequently associated with
northern barbarians (probably a logical offshoot of the idea that
they were unusually big), so the Batavians get one over on the
Roman sailors by conforming to type. The same sort of artful
duplicity crops up when the Batavian cohorts deliberately set out
to cause trouble for the Roman general Hordeonius Flaccus:

> Instantly swelling with arrogant ferocity, they began to
> demand a grant to pay for their journey, double wages, and
> reinforced numbers for their cavalry (measures certainly
> promised by Vitellius). They were not seriously seeking to get
> them, but sought an excuse for rebellion.

Histories 4.19

Northern barbarians were traditionally supposed to have hot
tempers and a weakness for money, so the Batavians duly appear
to show these characteristics when in fact they have ulterior
motives. Civilis would have been proud of them.

Civilis continues to ham it up as a typical barbarian to his
own advantage. So, he gives orders for women and children
from the German tribes to be put at the rear of the battle-line as

'inducements to victory or to shame them, if they were beaten' (*Histories* 4.18). This is a German military custom described by Tacitus at *Germania* 7. Also, as Civilis draws up his troops, he puts the Batavians in the centre and lines up the German tribesmen on both sides 'so as to look more savage' (*Histories* 4.22). It is as if the Batavians, robustly trained in Roman military techniques, are there to do the real fighting, while the others are present to create visual impact in a kind of psychological warfare. They even bring with them from their shrines the 'images of wild beasts', a practice which Tacitus describes at *Germania* 7. This pattern of showmanship is repeated during a night-battle at the siege of Vetera, when Civilis entrusts to the Batavians the engines and siege-works (the serious job), while he sets the German tribesmen a different task:

> Once the Germans from across the Rhine, clamouring for battle, were beaten off, he ordered them to demolish the rampart and renew the fighting. After all, they were a teeming horde and their losses hardly mattered.
>
> *Histories* 4.28

The idea of the 'barbarian horde', numerically superior but tactically weaker, is another feature of the ethnographical tradition. On top of that, the German tribesmen oblige with the appropriate variety of barbarian conduct, building fires, feasting and drinking and then rashly charging into battle (*Histories* 4.29). German fondness for wine is proverbial and features at *Germania* 23. It is almost as if the devious Civilis and his Batavians are using the *Germania* as a kind of handbook to display to the Romans as many instances of 'typical German behaviour' as possible, with the real German tribesmen available to add conviction to this charade.

The fundamentally disturbing thing about Civilis from a Roman perspective, as Tacitus makes clear, is his duality. He is both an enemy from within, trained in Roman fighting techniques and knowledgeable about their vulnerabilities, as well as an outsider, a Batavian nobleman, who can draw on his heritage as a non-Roman to stir collective feelings against an imperial power. Certain significant moments allow Tacitus to dramatise the murky nature of the war especially vividly. So, after the Roman soldiers from the legionary camp at Vetera surrender, only to be treacherously massacred by the Germans, Tacitus says:

> Civilis, who had taken a barbarian oath once the war against the Romans had started, had his wild and reddened hair cut off, now that the slaughter of the legions had at last been achieved.
>
> *Histories* 4.61

Civilis' haircut recalls a rite of passage described elsewhere by Tacitus in connection with a German tribe, the Chatti, whereby the men only cut their hair once they have killed an enemy in battle (*Germania* 31). Innocent German onlookers would therefore have been able to read Civilis' haircut as enacting a local tradition, although the context of the vow at the same time reveals the Batavian general's devious nature. The slaughter of the Roman legionaries, not in pitched battle, but treacherously after their surrender, is hardly the affirmation of manhood implicit in the rite of passage as described by Tacitus in the *Germania*. Indeed, Civilis himself, called by the Romans to account for this outrageous breaking of a promise, complains that it was the German tribesmen who ambushed the Roman column and that he had no control over them. Tacitus does not know what to believe: 'There is no evidence to show whether this was a pretence or whether he was really unable to restrain his savage troops' (*Histories* 4.60). It is important to see how in Tacitus this whole incident is riddled with themes of lies, treachery and uncertainty, because the hair-cutting scene will be emotively re-invented in the Dutch tradition.

In the end, Civilis' revolt is finally overwhelmed by its own burgeoning scale, as Gallic states join in and a multiplicity of leaders cause the whole venture to fragment, because of their widely differing aims and personal ambitions. It is this, more than any Roman intervention, which really makes the difference. In a decisive battle which takes place on familiar ground, the site of the ignominious massacre of Romans near the legionary camp at Vetera, the Romans finally defeat Civilis, whose energetic barbarian role-playing collapses. His devious personality and tricky techniques of leadership seem to be mirrored in the very landscape, described as 'treacherous with its precarious shadows and difficult for our men' (*Histories* 5.14). The Roman legionaries are inevitably not comfortable in this environment, and their fortunes are only revived by the timely intervention of a Batavian deserter, who shows the Roman general where to outflank the Germans by sending his cavalry over solid ground at the edge of the marshy terrain. It is strangely apt that Civilis, the 'Batavian turncoat' (*Histories* 4.21), has the tables turned on him by another 'Batavian turncoat' (*Histories* 5.18).

We can see how Tacitus' Civilis is above all deceptive and treacherous, and surrounds himself with obligingly devious Batavians (former Roman auxiliaries), who in turn magnify the tricky characteristics of their leader. As a historian, Tacitus probably had powerful reasons for choosing this emphasis, in that it subverts the 'official' version: those historical sources which broadly supported the victors in the civil war, the new Flavian regime, no doubt needed to play down the idea that this whole Batavian revolt had been irresponsibly triggered by Vespasian's supporters to help them win the civil war. Such pro-Flavian accounts would thus prefer to cast Julius Civilis more straightforwardly as a Germanic freedom-fighter, rather than as an 'enemy within', generated by the civil wars. Even the very last time that we see Tacitus' Civilis, when the text of the *Histories* breaks off, he stands dramatically on the end of a broken bridge across the river Nabalia, negotiating with the Roman general, Petilius Cerialis, perched on the other side (*Histories* 5.26). The irrepressible Julius Civilis, always with his eye on the main chance, tries to exploit his liminal status to the last by arguing that in fact, he had been fighting for Vespasian all along. With that, Civilis' story runs out, but it is a powerful reminder of his essentially tricky nature in Tacitus' account.

Julius Civilis emerges as a product of his troubled times, and as a tangible consequence of kaleidoscopic civil wars, where deception, treachery and pretence dominate the proceedings at every turn. On the face of it, Tacitus' legacy does not seem to offer much scope for the creation of a stirring national hero, but that did not stop Civilis and his Batavians from being appropriated by ingenious Dutch humanists in the sixteenth century, particularly once printed editions of Tacitus' texts started to become widely available. Yet the re-discovery of the *Histories* would not on its own have been enough to make Civilis rise like a phoenix from the ashes. What is crucial is that the Dutch intelligentsia began to engage with Tacitus' narrative at a period when they were increasingly concerned with their own identity, language and past, thanks in part to the dominant powers which controlled the region and encroached upon them. The presence of these 'outsiders' increasingly prompted the Dutch states to start considering their own origins and history, which was now being overshadowed. Since the fifteenth century, the whole area had been under the control of the Dukes of Burgundy, but during the early sixteenth century, it would pass into the hands of an even more formidable power, Charles V (1500-58), the Hapsburg emperor. When Charles V granted control of Spain and the Netherlands to his son, Philip II (1527-98), that oppressive regime triggered a prolonged Dutch war of independence (1568-1648), led initially by William of Orange (1533-84). In this context, if Civilis had not existed, somebody would have had to invent him.

During the sixteenth century, therefore, the concept of a 'Batavian past', convincingly rooted in antiquity, became an attractive device, which increasingly served the needs of the times. The first to mention the Batavians was a politician from Groningen, Wilhelmus Frederici, in his *About the Site of Frisia and the Origin of her People* (*de Frisiae situ gentisque origine* 1498), although he did so without trying to situate the Batavians in any specific locale. The trailblazer in that respect was Cornelius Aurelius (*c.* 1460-1531), a cleric from Gouda, who made detailed claims about the Batavians' homeland and thus suggested a coveted ancient ancestry for their 'descendants'. In his *Defence of Batavian Glory* (*Defensorium gloriae Batauinae* 1508, first draft), he proposed that the Batavians had originally settled in the county of Holland, and he followed up this initial study with *Explanation of Difficult Questions about the Batavian Region and its Distinctive Nature* (*Elucidarium scopulosarum quaestionum super Batauina regione et differentia* 1509-10). Both of these works were in Latin and addressed questions that were often recondite and complex, but the general message was still forceful: the ancient Batavians were the immediate forefathers of the Dutch, and these outside powers were therefore dealing with a people who had a long heritage and needed to be treated with respect. In this connection, an intriguing discovery was made in 1502 in the ruins of a Roman fortress south of Leiden. Two Latin inscriptions were found, one of which read: 'The Batavian people, brothers and friends of the Roman empire'. It turned out that this inscription was actually a fake, but the fact that somebody had bothered to concoct it in the first place is important: not only did it lay claim to the county of Holland as the centre of the ancient Batavian state, but it also projected a political message. If the Romans treated the Batavians as friends and brothers, rather than as subjects, then surely their descendants deserved the same treatment from powerful nations now?

The publication of Beraldo's 're-united' *Annals* in 1515 added further fuel to the fire, in that Tacitus' discussion of the island of the Batavians (*Annals* 2.6) now provided extra material to incorporate in the debate (which had so far focused on material from the *Histories* and *Germania*). This opened the way for a spirited challenge to Aurelius' claims from Gerardus Geldenhauer (*c.* 1482-1542), a native of Nijmegen, whose *Meditations about the Island of the Batavians* (*Lucubratiuncula de Batauorum insula c.* 1515-16), again in Latin, argued that the Batavians had actually settled in an area between the Rhine and the Maas, now belonging to the duchy of Guelders. The

Batavians thus became a focal point for expression of local rivalry between Guelders and Holland, played out in the pages of books written in Latin. The stakes got rather bigger when Aurelius reinforced his earlier argument about the provenance of the Batavians in his *Chronicles of Holland, Zeeland and Friesland* (*Die Cronycke van Hollandt, Zeelandt ende Vrieslant* 1517), written in the vernacular for the Dutch layman and introducing for good measure an eponymous Batavian settler named Battus. This work is also notable for being the first to incorporate the story of Civilis in the narrative, albeit in an abridged fashion, including his participation in a battle at Bonn (Figure 1). Tacitus narrates this clash, although Civilis

Figure 1. Battle at Bonn, from Cornelius Aurelius, *Chronicles of Holland, Zeeland and Friesland* (1517).

109

does not actually appear in the fighting in his version (*Histories* 4.20). Aurelius also tried to make his narrative more palatable for his rather different new readership by incorporating picturesque material drawn from Tacitus' *Germania*. The Batavians were now located in a timeless, innocent, arcadian society, dominated by systems of honour and subsisting on an agrarian economy. Yet in the end, Aurelius appears to have beaten off his challenger, so that Holland emerged as the 'victor' in the race to give the Batavians a homeland, but Geldenhauer stayed in the game by offering a fuller account of Battus (now called Baeto) in his *Batavian History* (*Historia Batauica* 1530). These early stages in the evolution of the Batavian myth are arguably concerned primarily with establishing the provenance of a people, but the exploratory focus on Baeto and Civilis is a sign of things to come.

When the Dutch revolt against the Spanish Hapsburg emperor broke out in 1568, the incipient 'Batavian myth' took on a new lease of life, since the contemporary rebellion was perceived to have powerful resonances with the earlier one, in which the romanticised rebel Civilis struggled to throw off Roman control. Writers quickly drew emotive connections between Civilis and their own rebel leader, William of Orange, and between the nations who were being challenged in each revolt, Rome and Spain. The combination of innocent arcadian Batavians and their charismatic leader Civilis offered an uplifting model for the Dutch struggle against Spain, even legitimising the revolt. At one point, Hugo Grotius published a legal defence of the revolt against Spain, *About the Antiquity of the Batavian State* (*de antiquitate reipublicae Batauicae* 1610), in which he used the ancient

Batavians to make arguments about the contemporary Dutch situation. It was written in Latin, but was soon followed by a vernacular translation. Its emphasis was on the egalitarian nature of the Batavian government, with assemblies debating the salient issues of the day, and if any supreme ruler was involved, he was there by common consent, rather than imposing his will from above. Such proliferating images of Batavians only further stimulated people's appetite for their common Batavian past.

The Batavians and material related to them also became a focus of serious scholarship going on in the new universities. William of Orange had founded the University of Leiden in 1575, and Justus Lipsius (1547-1606), appointed as professor history and law in 1579, turned his attention to Tacitus, the authority for so much of the Batavian material. Lipsius became one of Tacitus' most important early editors, commenting directly and patriotically in one of his editions on Civilis' role as a defender of public liberty. Civilis, as a Batavian 'hero', was a particular source of pride for him. That pride in a Batavian heritage extended far beyond Justus Lipsius and the University of Leiden. Thus, in 1619, when the Dutch under Jan Pieterszoon Coen conquered Djakarta in Indonesia, the city was obliged to change its name to Batavia, upon instructions from the directors of the Dutch East India Company. Hand-in-hand with Civilis in this rise to prominence went Baeto, the eponymous founder of the Batavians. In 1617, the gentleman poet Pieter Corneliszoon Hooft (who had also translated Tacitus) wrote his tragedy *Baeto*, casting Baeto as some latterday Aeneas, driven from his home amongst the Chatti to found a glorious new state:

There you will found a nation
That will last through all the centuries;
Batavians first will be their name,
Hollanders later, together with their new neighbours:
And they shall excel in peace and war, in everything
Always.

                Baeto 1429-33; based on I. Schöffer's translation

Such confident 'predictions' of a glorious future for Baeto's descendants reinforced their sense of self during the prolonged struggle against Hapsburg control. Civilis was a man whose noble resistance of the Romans (whatever the emphasis of Tacitus' original account) served as a model for the future, and we see him pictured on the frontispiece of Pontanus' *History of Guelders* (*Historiae Gelricae* 1639), flanking the title of the work, together with William of Orange (Figure 2). When the Dutch revolt eventually ended in 1648 and the Spanish finally recognised the sovereignty of the Dutch republic in the Peace of Münster, there was a celebratory pageant in Amsterdam, which had six *tableaux vivants* of Civilis and his rebellion as the centrepiece. Even long after the revolt ended, there was continuing interest in Civilis, for instance in Joost van den Vondel's *Batavian Brothers, or Suppressed Liberty* (*Batauische Gebroeders, of Onderdruckte Vryheit* 1663). In composing this tragedy, van den Vondel professed that he had been inspired by thirty-six etchings of Civilis created by the Italian artist Antonio Tempestata early in the century.

The visual arts certainly showed just as much interest in Civilis as the literary world. Between 1600 and 1610, the painter Otto van Veen, also inspired by Tempestata's etchings, produced twelve edifying paintings of significant moments from Civilis'

Figure 2. Civilis and William of Orange on the title-page of Pontanus'
History of Guelders (1639).

rebellion, including scenes based on the initial swearing of oaths to establish the confederation and Civilis' symbolic hair-cutting (Figure 3). These he sold to the States General in The Hague in 1613 as appropriately inspiring images for the assembly chamber. That precedent later put an idea into the heads of the town council of Amsterdam, who decided to commission Civilis-related paintings for their new town hall. With the sudden death of their first artist, Govert Flick, in 1660, the councillors, keen to get the job done, decided to hedge their bets by commissioning separate painters to produce four enormous works (each 28 metres square). The first to be taken on were Jacob Jordaens and Jan Lievens: the former, who produced two paintings, chose as his subject-matter the Batavian attack on

Figure 3. Otto van Veen, *Civilis has his Hair Cut* (before 1612); Tacitus *Histories* 4.61. Rijksmuseum, Amsterdam.

the Roman camp at night (*Histories* 4.28-30) and the restoration of the old alliance between Romans and Batavians (*Histories* 5.26), while the latter depicted Civilis' associate, Brinno, being raised on a shield (Tacitus *Histories* 4.15). Rembrandt (1606-69), commissioned slightly later, opted for the initial swearing of oaths in the forest, although he set the scene at a banqueting table, with the one-eyed Civilis holding up a sword against which his co-conspirators are placing their own swords to symbolise the pact (*Histories* 4.14-15).

With the paintings finished and in place in the town hall, that should have been the end of it. Yet something happened: in 1662, Rembrandt's painting was removed, to be replaced instead with a touched-up version of one of Flick's original unfinished works. Rembrandt's painting (Figure 4) was later sold to a private client, and was greatly reduced in size to show only a portion of the original work, perhaps modified by the artist himself or by a later owner. The reasons for the painting's removal are unclear and still generate lively debate today. Was the monumental work displeasing to the town council for aesthetic reasons? The suggestion has been made that Rembrandt's graphic depiction of Civilis' damaged eye-socket, not so far a traditional feature of such paintings, may have proved too much. Indeed, the whole painting perhaps pushed the boundaries too far, in that its rebels were menacing outcasts, rather than civilised freedom-fighters who fought the Romans because they had to, but ultimately wanted a reconciliation with the Romans (depicted in one of Jordaens' paintings). Rembrandt had perhaps read his text of Tacitus a little too carefully for the prevailing tastes of the Amsterdam town council. Or was the problem some sort of double-meaning embedded in

115

the subject-matter of the painting? Some have speculated that Civilis' imposing head-gear suggests an almost regal figure, rather than the egalitarian 'first amongst equals' rebel leader, who had become popular as the Batavian myth evolved. The height suggested by the hat (whether or not it implies a crown) and the effects with the lighting draw the eye to Civilis and place him on a level above his fellow-conspirators. No doubt the theories about this controversial painting will continue to fly around, but its removal from the town hall in Amsterdam shows that romanticised perceptions of Civilis had come a long way from Tacitus' original, rather grubby creation in the *Histories*. 'Civilis' now had a life of his own that his creator could hardly have predicted when he shaped his version of the historical Civilis.

Figure 4. Rembrandt, *The Oath of Civilis* (1661). Nationalmuseum, Stockholm.

3. From Hellraisers to Heroes

Arminius and the Germans

The Cheruscan rebel Arminius, who famously massacred three of Augustus' legions in AD 9 in the Teutoburg forest, attracted a more sustained interest from Classical authors than Julius Civilis did, at least in those texts from antiquity that survive. Yet he still has a great deal in common with the leader of the Batavian revolt, in that by far the most subtle and elaborate literary portrait of the man was created by Tacitus in the first two books of the *Annals*. Moreover, Arminius, in much the same way as Civilis, had an extraordinarily rich afterlife, once he was eagerly appropriated as a powerful national symbol after the rediscovery of Tacitus' texts. The transformation of Tacitus' complex and flawed Arminius into a more perfect version of his former self can be seen to mirror the reception of Civilis by the Dutch in the sixteenth and seventeenth centuries, which is one reason for setting the pair side by side in this chapter.

The ancient literary tradition outside Tacitus tends to portray Arminius in a freeze-frame manner, without exploring his inner feelings and motivations for revolt. The first writer to present Arminius is the geographer Strabo, whose account was written (or revised) early in Tiberius' principate, while the rebel leader was still at large after his attack on Augustus' legions. Strabo uses the example of Arminius' tribe, the Cherusci, as the archetype of faithless Germans:

> Those natives who have been trusted have inflicted the greatest harm, such as the Cherusci and their subjects. At their hands, three Roman legions with their general Quintilius Varus were destroyed in an ambush, and a treaty was broken. They all paid

the penalty and provided the younger Germanicus with a most glittering triumph. In this triumphal procession went their most illustrious men and women: Segimuntus, son of Segestes and general of the Cherusci, his sister named Thusnelda, wife of Arminius (the one who was leader of the Cherusci when they broke faith with Quintilius Varus and who even now is continuing the war), as well as her three-year-old son, Thumelicus. Also present were Sesithacus, the son of Segimerus, general of the Cherusci, and his wife, Rhamis, a daughter of Ucromirus, who was general of the Chatti, and Deudorix, a Sugumbrian who was the son of Baetorix, the brother of Melo. Segestes, Arminius' father-in-law, dissented from that man's scheme even from the very beginning, and seizing the moment, deserted him and was present in the triumph involving his dearest ones, he himself being treated with honour.

Geography 7.1.4

In this description, Strabo moves with dazzling speed from the destruction of Varus' legions in AD 9 to Germanicus' glittering triumph of AD 17, in which most of the Cheruscan nobility appear as captives; and the level of details in providing names and family heritage fosters the mood of optimism. The Roman general Varus, blamed elsewhere for his reckless assumption that he had nothing to fear from these 'pacified' tribes, is cast as an unfortunate victim of this treaty-breaking group. And Arminius himself is not mentioned in the context of the ambush, but is kept waiting in the wings until his unfortunate wife appears in the triumphal procession. He is therefore side-lined and subordinated to a captive woman, all of which makes his continuing efforts to fight the Romans seem rather futile, given what has already happened to his family (one of whom turned his back on the man even while the ambush was at the planning stage). Strabo uses such strategies to deflate Arminius, who duly disappears from the narrative after this brief appearance, and to overlay disaster reassuringly with triumph. The poet Ovid goes one better. In a description of an imaginary triumph over Germany, he points to one conspicuous figure: 'This traitor trapped our men in an ambush which took advantage of the terrain, the one who now covers his unkempt face with his long hair' (*Tristia* 4.2.33-4). Ovid does not explicitly name Arminius, but this is surely the intended point of reference. The public humiliation in a triumphal procession never happened, but it is the next step up from Strabo inserting a potted sketch of Arminius into the triumph featuring his family and thus firmly putting him in his place. Ovid diverges from Strabo in the hint of emotion attributed to his German rebel, who covers his face with his long hair to block out the gleeful gaze of the victorious Romans, but that detail creates a sense of vindication, rather than pity.

The next surviving description of Arminius comes in the Roman historian Velleius Paterculus, who lived under Tiberius and had actually spent AD 4-12 on military service in Germany. That potentially made him an important witness, but he does not allow his personal experience to get in the way of a rhetorically embellished account. His narrative of the the ambush is unusually long, considering that this is a summary of the whole of Roman history, but this is because he uses it as a suitably dark prelude to the positive intervention of Tiberius, 'the perpetual defender of the Roman empire' (*Roman History* 2.120). Velleius begins with a description of Varus' shortcomings and then moves on to characterise the Germans:

Those people – one would hardly believe this without having experienced it – are very cunning, despite their extreme wildness, and they are a race born to tell lies. By trumping up a succession of fake law-cases, now provoking one another to quarrels, now expressing gratitude that Roman justice was terminating those disputes, that their own wildness was being softened by the new experience of this unfamiliar learning, and that problems usually settled by fighting were being resolved by law, they led Varus to the utmost complacency, so much that he believed himself an urban praetor dispensing justice in the forum, not commander of an army right in the heart of Germany.

Roman History 2.118

Velleius here has to appeal to his personal experience of the area, in order to counteract the common assumption of his contemporary audience that all northern barbarians are stupid. This move must also be designed to deflect in advance at least some blame from the 'honest' Romans for falling into the ambush, although Varus himself is not spared from criticism. Indeed, Velleius clearly sets him up as a scapegoat, in a way that Strabo certainly did not.

Against this collective portrait of the tribe, Velleius places his lively character-sketch of Arminius:

Then there was a young man of noble birth, brave in action, quick-witted and clearly intelligent beyond what was usual for a barbarian. Arminius was his name, son of Sigimer, who was leader of that people, and he showed his passionate spirit in his face and in his eyes. He was a constant associate on our previous military campaign, and after actually gaining Roman

3. From Hellraisers to Heroes

citizenship and equestrian rank, he exploited the Roman
general's complacency as an opportunity for crime.

Roman History 2.118

Arminius' cleverness, deemed unusual in barbarians, paradoxically makes him typical in the immediate context, since his
people are just as quick-witted, as we have seen. Their charac-
teristic reflects on him, and he in turn reinforces the collective
portrait. And for a moment, he almost seems admirable, as his
passionate spirit shines out through his face, but Velleius brings
down the tone of the description with a bump. Not only is
Arminius a Roman auxiliary soldier, who has won prized citizenship and equestrian rank, but he also seems to know Varus
personally. Both factors make his imminent treacherous
conduct especially despicable. Velleius' Arminius, inhabiting
exactly the same sort of morally dubious twilight zone as
Tacitus' Julius Civilis, is a figure from the margins of the Roman
world, to whom privileges have been extended; but imminently,
he will bite the hand that feeds him.

Yet in Velleius' account of the ambush itself, Arminius is
rendered (unexpectedly) invisible. The emphasis instead is on
the folly of Varus, who was even warned about the plot in
advance. However, the pro-Roman chieftain Segestes, like
Cassandra, is not believed, and disaster follows. During the
attack, Arminius is not mentioned at all, and references
instead are to 'the enemy', indicating the Germans collectively. Arminius is simply erased from the cataclysmic event,
surprisingly so, given the fanfare with which Velleius introduced him. Perhaps Velleius was reserving a fuller version of
the disaster for an extended history, a project which he

mentions more than once, but that alone does not explain Arminius' invisibility. Perhaps it was a strategy for neutralising atavistic Roman fears about the event and pulling down to size the most famous 'hero' of the Cherusci. Strabo had done something similar by side-stepping a detailed description of the ambush and concentrating instead on the Roman triumph.

If we turn to other relevant accounts, the same phenomenon is in evidence. Cassius Dio, writing in the third century AD, gives an atmospheric account of the events in the forest, but sets up the conflict very much in terms of collective protagonists, Romans versus Germans (56.20-1). As in Velleius' version, Arminius' role as an individual leader has been compressed and circumscribed within a much broader account of failed Roman imperialism and collective German treachery. We see the same absence of Arminius from the ambush itself in the late Latin writer, Florus (*Epitome of Roman History* 2.30), who mentions him only once. It is of course possible that these surviving accounts are unrepresentative, and that other versions, now lost, assigned Arminius a more central role. Yet it may be that what we are seeing here is a kind of self-censorship in the collective memory: everyone knew what Arminius had done, so there was no need to rub salt in the wound by actively depicting him slaughtering Romans in the forest. Whatever the explanation, the most conspicuous point about non-Tacitean versions of the massacre is that the activities of the leader Arminius are not depicted. The only exception is a brief snapshot in Frontinus, in a section of his work which assembles examples of how to conclude a war after a successful engagement:

Arminius, general of the Germans, ordered that the heads of those whom he had killed should likewise be impaled on spears and brought up to the rampart of the enemy.

Stratagems 2.8.4

This is a memorable strategy for demoralising an opponent, but hardly equates to an extended description of an ambush.

Outside Tacitus' *Annals*, Arminius remains a marginalised figure, two-dimensional and shallow, with no speculation about his motives for turning his back on the Romans. At best, he is characterised as a resourceful opportunist, too clever by half for a barbarian, and at worst, a traitor, who deviously used his personal knowledge of Varus and the Roman military system to unleash a devastating attack. Nothing is said anywhere about his death, even in terms of grim satisfaction that this traitor was finally eliminated through his own relatives' treachery. If these other accounts were all that survived, it seems unlikely that the tarnished Arminius would have been turned into such a vibrant figure in years to come, and he indeed may have been completely forgotten. Tacitus was the one responsible for his survival. This is quite a surprise, if we consider that Arminius' acme was the slaughter of Varus' legions in AD 9, and Tacitus' *Annals* pointedly begins with the accession of Tiberius in AD 14.

Arminius' story in Tacitus is complex and peppered over two books of the *Annals*. He first appears after an announcement of a triumph bestowed upon the Roman general Germanicus in AD 15 for a war in Germany which had not been finished. This is a nicely suggestive touch, hinting at *hybris* in the Romans, who surely cannot afford, in Germany of all places, to be so complacent:

123

For hope had arisen that the enemy was divided between Arminius and Segestes, each famous for his disloyalty or loyalty towards us. Arminius was the troublemaker of Germany. Segestes often revealed that rebellion was on the cards, especially at that last banquet, after which they took up arms; and he urged Varus to place Arminius, himself and the other chieftains under arrest, (arguing that) the people would not dare to make a move once their leaders had been removed, and that Varus would have time to separate the guilty and the innocent. However, Varus fell victim to fate and Arminius' violence. Segestes, although dragged into the war by the consensus of his people, remained disaffected, after his hatred had been intensified privately because Arminius had seized his daughter, who had been promised to another man. The son-in-law was resented by his hostile father-in-law, and a relationship which forms an affectionate bond between those in harmony proved an incitement to angry feelings between opponents.

Annals 1.55

This introduction has some similarities with the accounts of Arminius which we have considered so far, particularly in the sketchy reference to the massacre of AD 9, which is swiftly glossed over, and in the complacency of Varus, who completely ignores Segestes' warning. Yet there are also some innovations. Tacitus uniquely elaborates and fleshes out the family feud between Arminius and Segestes. Strabo had mentioned the basic disagreement, but without attributing motives to either party. Tacitus implicitly humanises Arminius as a passionate man, who is prepared to steal a woman betrothed to somebody else, whatever the consequences. This is much more specific than Velleius' general reference to Arminius' passionate spirit shining from his face. It also constitutes an unusual attempt to recapture the internal dynamics operating amongst the Cheruscan elite, bucking the Romanocentric tendencies of most other analyses. Behind the straightforwardly pro- and anti-Roman stances of Segestes and Arminius lies a personal quarrel, and the possibility that at least one, and perhaps both, could be using politics to pursue their private disputes. Gone are the broad descriptive tags reminiscent of the ethnographical tradition that these people are 'pretty clever for barbarians'. Their deviousness takes a different form. So, when Segestes, rescued by Germanicus from a siege conducted against him by his own people, and reviewing his past services to the Romans, he claims that he told Varus about Arminius in the belief that peace was in the best interests of Romans and Germans:

> It was for that reason that I denounced the plunderer of my daughter, the violator of your treaty, Arminius, as a defendant before Varus, who was then in charge of the army.
>
> *Annals* 1.58

His scornful tag for Arminius as the plunderer of his daughter reminds us that despite those fine words about shared Roman and German interests, it is actually his domestic dispute with Arminius that prompted him to act. This hatred is despite the fact that the daughter herself – pregnant in Tacitus' account – is depicted as devoted to her husband (*Annals* 1.57).

So far we have seen Arminius in rather a fragmented way, through the lenses of internal protagonists such as the hostile Segestes or through authorial glosses of his past actions from

Tacitus. Now finally, for the first time in any of our sources, he is allowed to speak for himself, and what he says and does is stirring stuff:

> Quite apart from his naturally violent temperament, Arminius was driven mad by his wife's capture and by the subjugation of her unborn child. He flew around the Cherusci, demanding war against Segestes, war against Caesar. He did not pull his punches: what a wonderful father, a great commander, a brave army, whose numerous hands had carried off one little woman! By contrast, he had laid low three legions and their legates. He did not conduct war by betrayal or against pregnant women, but openly against armed men. There could still be seen Roman standards in German groves, which he had put up for the gods of their country. Let Segestes live on the conquered river-bank, let him restore to his son an abandoned priesthood. Germans would never sufficiently excuse the fact that between the Elbe and the Rhine, they had seen Roman rods and axes, and the toga. To other races, ignorant of Roman power, the punishments were unknown, the taxes unfamiliar …. If they preferred their fatherland, parents, and traditions to overlords and new colonies, they should follow Arminius' lead to glory and freedom, rather than Segestes to disgraceful slavery.
>
> *Annals* 1.59

The blistering language sweeps us up, but it should not blind us to the fact that Arminius makes some distinctly odd claims. His fury at the capture of his pregnant wife leads him, for instance, to claim that he, at least, fights openly without resorting to treachery. This is palpably untrue, coming from the mouth of someone who had betrayed Varus in such startling circum-

stances and whose main claim to fame was a devious ambush of
Roman troops in the depths of a forest. And since most of his
speech is taken up with expressing outrage about his captured
wife, a personal issue, his switch to a public stance at the end,
with his climactic call to liberty, raises questions about his
sincerity. Is Arminius really set on freeing the Germans from
Roman shackles, or is he just using his compatriots to pursue a
private feud? The tendency for calls to liberty to be appropriated
by the devious prompted the Roman general Cerialis to observe:

> The Germans always have the same reasons for crossing over to
> Gaul, namely lust, greed and desire to change their homeland,
> so that after leaving these marshes and lonely places, they can
> get their hands on this most fertile terrain – and on you too.
> Yet 'freedom' and other specious buzzwords are used as a
> pretext. Nobody has ever coveted slavery for others and
> supreme power for himself without appropriating those very
> same terms.
>
> *Histories* 4.73

Is that sort of game going on here with Arminius? Other
accounts simply classify him as duplicitous, but in Tacitus he
has a more elusive identity, with the balance between public and
private motivations left murky and unclear. Yet his forceful
language and passion still prompts us to admire him, despite his
past actions, although a contemporary Roman response may
well have been ambivalent.

The ghostly spirits of Varus and his legions are always lurking
in the background whenever Arminius features in the narrative,
but nowhere more so than in the scene where the Roman

general Caecina is leading his men back to the River Ems after their dutiful burial of Varus' soldiers, six years after the original massacre (*Annals* 1.61-8). Tacitus knows the emotive power of events which take place on the same site as previous incidents, and he incorporates such territorial 'doublets' elsewhere, particularly in a military context: so, in *Histories* 2 and 3, there are the two central battles of the civil war which take place on the same site near Bedriacum in northern Italy, and there is also the clash between Romans and Germans in *Histories* 5.14-18, which unfolds near the abandoned legionary camp at Vetera, the location of an earlier notorious massacre of Romans (*Histories* 4.60). Such scenes have the potential either to repeat or reverse the past, and on that basis, they can engage readers in a particularly gripping way. The visit to the site of Varus' diasaster by Germanicus and his men is arguably one of the most eerie in Tacitus, and it is a brilliant way to incorporate in the narrative a set of events, which formally lie outside the chronological parameters of the work:

First, Varus' camp, with its wide perimeter and carefully measured out headquarters, showed the hard work of the three legions. Then, behind a half-destroyed rampart and a shallow ditch, the survivors, now under attack, had apparently gathered together. In the middle of the plain, the whitening bones were scattered or piled up, depending on whether they had fled or taken a stand. Pieces of weapons and horses' limbs lay close at hand, and likewise on the trunks of trees, skulls were secured. In nearby groves were barbarian altars, at which they had sacrificed tribunes and centurions of leading ranks. Survivors of that disaster, who had escaped battle or capture, recalled that here the legates had fallen, there the eagles had been seized; that was where Varus' first wound had been inflicted, when he had found death by a blow from his unlucky right hand; there was the platform at which Arminius had delivered his harangue, and that was how many gibbets there had been for the captives and those were the pits, and they recalled how Arminius had arrogantly mocked the military standards and the eagles.

Annals 1.61

As the focus slides from gruesome present to the terrifying past, thanks to the vivid memories of the survivors who interpret the remains, Tacitus uniquely places Arminius centre-stage in the massacre, orchestrating the deaths around him and heaping further degradation on Roman soldiers, who are already intensely humiliated. Our other sources gloss over such horrors, but Tacitus uses the powerful historiographical device of memory to 'reinstate' Arminius as the chilling embodiment of the vindictive enemy. The past seems to come alive before our very eyes, and it continues to do so after the Romans leave the site. The Roman general Caecina has a haunting dream, in which Varus, smeared with blood, rises from the swamp and beckons him to come and join him (*Annals* 1.65), and on the following day, when Arminius orders his men to attack, he completes the fusion of past and present by shouting, 'Look! Varus and his legions bound up again by the same fate!' (*Annals* 1.65).

Yet all of these suggestive markers do not, in the event, result in a straightforward repetition of the past. This time there are two German commanders, Arminius and his uncle Inguiomerus, who disagree on the appropriate strategy, and the Romans manage to exploit (what turns out to be) misleading self-confidence amongst the Germans, so sure that their current enemy will be easy pickings, just like the last lot. Yet the Roman general Caecina is far more competent than Varus was, and the Germans are now vulnerable precisely because the Romans know about their techniques from Arminius' success in AD 9. The whole sequence suggests that Tacitus' Arminius is not as versatile as his reputation would suggest. He fights by taking advantage of the terrain and incapacitating Roman military techniques through the forest locale, but he has weaknesses. Tensions with other German leaders can obstruct him, just as much as decent opposition from the Romans; and Caecina's achievement in beating the Germans on this occasion means that the next time Arminius tries to raise the spectre of Varus in a battle (*Annals* 2.15, 2.45), it has a little less impact. Instead of being rousing, it begins to sounds rather desperate, the cry of a leader resting on his laurels.

In practical terms, Arminius is not the force that he once was, but he persists in his efforts against the Romans. In one memorable scene, he confronts his one-eyed brother Flavus, who has been fighting for Germanicus in the Roman army (*Annals* 2.9-10). They meet on opposite sides of the river Visurgis: Flavus talks in terms of Roman greatness, the wealth of the emperor, the grave punishments for the defeated and the prospects of mercy for those who concede, while Arminius dwells on patriotism, ancestral freedon and the native gods of Germany, proudly equating his own efforts with liberty and regarding his brother as nothing more than a slave. The polarisation is undercut to some extent because they talk in Latin, 'since Arminius had previously served in the Roman camp as a commander of the Cheruscan auxiliaries' (*Annals* 2.10). It is almost as if Arminius, in facing Flavus, is looking at an image of his own past, before he became a freedom-fighter, as well as at his own alternative present, if he had not massacred Varus' legions in AD 9. The scene between the two brothers reminds us of the grubby turn-coat Arminius of the literary tradition, just when he is most conspicuously not aligned with that negative version of himself.

It would have been so easy for Tacitus to paint Arminius straightforwardly as the treacherous enemy from within, much as he did with the manipulative Julius Civilis in the *Histories*, but instead we get a leader who embraces concepts of liberty at significant moments and who continues to struggle against the Romans, even when it would have been more practical to desist. We even feel admiration for him at times, because of his passion and charisma. Like the Roman general Germanicus, Arminius seems to hark back to earlier times, when the republic faced formidable enemies, who really challenged them. For a figure who generates such universal loathing and fear in the collective Roman consciousness, Tacitus' Arminius is cast in a surprisingly positive light. His depiction is not completely devoid of darker tones, but the subtle and complex characterisation makes him three-dimensional and real in a way that contrasts sharply with the lifeless caricatures provided by our other sources. Once Arminius' powers have dwindled, after a defeat by Germanicus (*Annals* 2.11-18) and escalation of internal conflicts with Maroboduus, king of the Suebi (*Annals* 2.44-6), Tacitus' final obituary is eloquent:

However, Arminius, as the Romans were withdrawing and Maroboduus had been beaten, aimed at kingship and came face to face with his people's love of liberty. He became the target of their arms and fought with varying degrees of success, but fell by the treachery of his kinsmen. He was the liberator of Germany without a doubt, and a man who challenged not the first beginnings of the Roman people, as other kings and generals did, but a most flourishing empire. Indecisive in battles, but unconquered in war, he lived for thirty-seven years and held power for twelve of these. Songs are still sung about him amongst barbarian tribes, although he is unknown to the annals of the Greeks, who only marvel at their own deeds, while he is not properly celebrated in Roman writers, since we respect antiquity, but neglect recent history.

Annals 2.88

Tacitus' impatient reprimand of other Roman writers is of course a familiar literary strategy to enhance the standing of his own work by contrast, but his extensive treatment of Arminius seems genuinely innovative. Even if other lost histories (such as those of Pliny the Elder and Aufidius Bassus) offered their own portraits of Arminius, Tacitus' creation is the one which invested the 'liberator of Germany' with touches of heroism and laid the groundwork for his enthusiastic reception centuries later. What follows is a selection of highlights from an extremely vibrant tradition about Arminius (so vibrant in fact that one really has to be selective).

In the fifteenth century, German humanists such as Conrad Celtis (1459-1508) had quickly taken up Tacitus' *Germania* (first printed in 1470) as a powerful weapon in their disputes with the Papacy, urgently appealing to national pride through revived images of the innocent, warlike ancient Germans, who (unlike the Gauls and others) had remained unconquered by the Romans. Yet the publication of the complete text of the *Annals* in 1515 saw a fresh (and timely) element enter the debate, in the form of a tangible individual hero, Arminius. That was something that the *Germania*, with its collective focus on tribal groups, could not provide. It was Ulrich von Hutten (1488-1523), the fiery German humanist and poet, who set in motion Arminius' vibrant afterlife as a focus for German national pride. Soon after Martin Luther had momentously attached to the door of the church in Wittenberg his ninety-five theses challenging the right of the papacy to sell indulgences (1517), a move which initiated the Protestant Reformation, Hutten sat down to create his dialogue *Arminius*, written in Latin in 1519 or 1520 and published posthumously in 1529. It was inspired both by Tacitus' *Annals* and also by Lucian's twelfth *Dialogue of the Dead* (where the dead generals Alexander the Great, Scipio and Hannibal debate which of them can lay claim to be the greatest; Minos pronounced Alexander the victor). The *Arminius* is an intensely patriotic work, celebrating Arminius' role as a freedom-fighter against Roman authority (now embodied by the Papacy for a contemporary audience) and suggesting that Arminius' descendants should follow his lead.

In one memorable sequence set in the underworld, Arminius challenges Minos' pronouncement that the greatest generals are Alexander the Great, Scipio the Elder and Hannibal (in that order) by asking Mercury to summon Tacitus from the Elysian fields to plead on his behalf. Arminius is particularly keen for Tacitus to use his obituary at *Annals* 2.88 as decisive evidence, and thanks to the authority of this respected and eloquent ancient author, Minos reinstates Arminius as the equal of the greatest generals. It is striking that Hutten makes Arminius argue forcefully that he was striving for the liberty of his own people, and plays down the idea that he was driven by selfish or personal motives (a theme which Tacitus pursues in his focus on Arminius' quarrel with Segestes). Although the *Arminius* was written in Latin and was therefore accessible only to a relatively narrow circle of the educated, it put Arminius on the map as an ardent patriot endorsed by the credentials of antiquity and realised his potential as a character relevant to the contemporary political scene.

It took a reference from Martin Luther to Arminius as Herman in his discussion of Psalm 82 and a patriotic poem written in German to raise Arminius' profile and disseminate knowledge of him more widely. Burkhard Waldis (1490-1556) in his *Illustrated Rhyming Chronicle* (*Illustrierten Reimchronik* 1543) celebrated Arminius proudly:

> Arminius, whom they call Herman,
> A young hero, a bold man,
> Who grew up well in body and soul,
> Born in the Hartz, a prince of Saxony.

The Arminius seen here is more of an idealised general type than a nuanced and subtle character, but his transition from the closeted world of Latin to works accessible through German secured his fame and generated huge interest, which was expressed subsequently in a wealth of literature, drama and song (in both Latin and German). Arminius proved to be an enduring and versatile symbol. Nicodemus Frischlin (1547-90) even put him on the stage in a patriotic comedy, *Julius Caesar Back From the Dead* (*Julius Caesar Redivivus* 1584). In this play, engagingly riddled with anachronisms, the spirits of Caesar and Cicero go on a journey of exploration in sixteenth-century Germany, each accompanied by a travelling companion: Cicero takes along the humanist Eobanus Hessus, while Caesar (being a military man) has with him Arminius. The comedy has rather an Aristophanic feel to it, but the grand sightseeing tour is grounded in admiration for the social and cultural achievements of contemporary Germany.

On a more serious note, the playwright Johannes Rist (1607-67), wrote a pair of moralising dramas, *Peace-Wishing Germany* (*Das Friedewünschende Deutschland* 1647) and *Jubilant Germany* (*Das Friedejautchtzende Deutschland* 1653), inspired by the events of the Thirty Years' War (1618-48), which he cast as a divine punishment of Germany and as a mechanism for purifying her corrupt soul. Rist (probably inspired by Hutten) has Mercury serve as a guide for four ancient ghosts, Ariovistus, the barbarian leader made famous by Caesar, Duke Widukint of Saxony, who flourished under Charlemagne, and (a particularly interesting dual appearance), Julius Civilis, the Batavian rebel, and Arminius. Their collective role is to serve as arbiters, shocked at the contemporary state of Germany and at the squandering of their collective legacy by a morally bankrupt people.

The outburst of Arminius-related creativity continued in the form of a huge didactic novel by Daniel Casper von Lohenstein (1635-83), called *The Great-hearted General Arminius, or Hermann* (*Grossmüthiger Feldherr Arminius, oder Hermann* 1689), incomplete at the time of his death and published posthumously (but completed by another writer). It is a patriotic adventure story, albeit one fleshed out with an array of recondite details designed to educate his readers, and an enormous cast of characters. Only about four of the eighteen books are concerned directly with Arminius himself, who is surrounded by a host of other protagonists, including historical figures such as Varus, Segestes,

Thusnelda and Maroboduus, but also fictional creations, such as Arminius' sister, Ismene, and his mother, Asblaste, whose stories are also traced in miniature epic cycles. The whole monumental narrative (which embraces tales of shipwreck, imprisonment, mistaken identity, love-stories, divided families, and much more) is sprawling and complex, but it is bound together by a deeply-embedded awareness of a robust German heroic identity, which has the scope to overcome almost anything. The original edition of the novel included an impressive copper engraving of Arminius, decked out in armour and raising a tankard (Figure 5).

A rather different variety of creative expression can be found in a trilogy of plays written by the dramatist Friedrich Gottlieb Klopstock (1724-1803). *Hermann's Battle* (*Hermanns Schlacht* 1769), *Hermann and the Princes* (*Hermann und die Fürsten* 1784, although written much earlier in 1767) and the *Death of Hermann* (*Hermanns Tod* 1787) present loosely connected heroic panels of central moments from Arminius' life, interspersed with lyric inter-ludes, all of which are intended to pull together in an inspiring way to generate a sense of patriotic duty in his contemporaries, who should be prepared to sacrifice everything for their country. Characters other than Arminius appear to have undergone their own transformation in these plays: so, Brinno, the opportunistic supporter of Civilis' Batavian revolt in Tacitus, seems to have been transplanted to Klopstock's version of the Arminius story in the form of the fair-minded Brenno, a druidic high priest infused with the sort of wisdom which elsewhere is associated with wise old birds like Homer's Nestor. He delivers a harsh but fair judgement on the traitors, Segestes, his son Siegmund, and Arminius' brother Flavius, and serves as a mouthpiece for the poet's own moralising. Klopstock does not, for example, sidestep the problem of internal

Figure 5. Arminius in battle armour, holding a tankard, from Daniel Casper von Lohenstein, *The Great-hearted General Arminius* (1689).

discord amongst the Germans as a dangerous and divisive factor in politics, still relevant in his own day. Some of the themes have

137

a Homeric flavour about them, such as in the second play, when
Ingomar (Tacitus' Inguiomerus) opposes his nephew Hermann
because his sense of honour prevents him from submitting to a
younger man (however sensible the plan); or in the final play,
when even Hermann's Roman enemies feel pity for his fate.
Hermann's wife Thusnelda is especially powerfully drawn in all
the plays, especially the last. We can see this interest in the female
characters of the myth sustained in Karl von Piloty's monumental
painting, *Thusnelda in the Triumphal Procession of Germanicus*
(*Thusnelda im Triumphzug des Germanicus* 1873), which is a
proud expression of the robust nature of the German race, even
in oppressive circumstances (Figure 6). Yet although individual

Figure 6. Karl von Piloty, *Thusnelda in the Triumphal Procession of Germanicus*
(1873). Bayerische Staatsgemäldesammlungen, Munich.

scenes in Klopstick's plays are emotionally powerful (and the last play is probably the best), the trio of dramas seem to lack cohesiveness when considered as a whole, and as far as we know, the entire patriotic trilogy was never performed on stage.

While Klopstick's plays exhibit a sort of timeless patriotism, another drama about Arminius, *Hermann's Battle* (*Die Hermannsschlacht* 1808) by Heinrich von Kleist (1777-1811), was generated from the immediate political circumstances in which it was written. After Napoleon won the battle of Austerlitz (2 December 1805), in 1806 he became 'Protector' of the Rhine Confederation, which was intended to create a buffer zone between France and Prussia and to supply the empire with soldiers. For those rulers who complied, the rewards were tangible (and could include smaller states whose rulers were not so co-operative), but the whole arrangement jeopardised German freedom and identity, and encouraged collaboration with the 'protector' at the expense of helping one's fellow-countrymen. In this context, Kleist's *Hermann's Battle* is an urgent call to arms, written very much for the present as propaganda. So, where Klopstick in his trilogy underscored the devastating cost of internal German discord, Kleist played down that theme, which would have undermined German morale and thus been detrimental to the anti-Napoleonic message of the play. Well-established characters such as Arminius' collaborator brother Flavius have therefore been abandoned. Instead, Kleist focuses on Roman attempts to play off Hermann and Marbod (Tacitus' Maroboduus) against one another. The charismatic Hermann, however, is too clever for the Romans, and although he initially seems to play along, he secretly contacts his old enemy Marbod and the two men agree on a plan, which culminates in the massacre of Varus and his legions. At the end of the play, Hermann and Marbod clasp hands over the scattered corpses of the legionaries, projecting a powerful message of what a reunited Germany could achieve against the external enemy. Yet despite Kleist's passionate message, this potentially explosive play was never performed at the time it was written, and it was not even printed until 1861 (after which it became very popular indeed and was staged repeatedly). Kleist was bitterly disappointed and died in 1811 before the German states had been prised from Napoleon's grasp.

Not every reincarnation of Arminius was straightforwardly positive. Heinrich Heine (1797-1856) saw Arminius' potential for articulating a more critical response to the state of his contemporary Germany in his urbane satire, *Deutschland: A Winter's Tale* (*Deutschland: ein Wintermärchen* 1844). His targets in this vibrant and entertaining poem included misrule, censorship, the idle rich, militarism and excessive attachment to the past, destructive factors which were debilitating the country that he loved (and that affection comes through powerfully in the satire itself, which is full of fond appreciation of Germany's assets, whether in the form of excellent German hock or luxurious German feather-beds). The work was predictably banned in Germany, even though Heine had followed his publisher's advice in toning down some of the more contentious stanzas, and indeed it only circulated there at all because it had found a publisher in the Free City of Hamburg, although stocks were still confiscated whenever they were located. Heine was certainly an uncomfortable voice for the authorities to confront, and his poem, rooted in real life, but buoyed up by imaginative flights of fancy, has about it an infectious and highly readable quality.

His constant touches of humour are engaging, such as when he deflates the puffed up Prussian soldiers by poking fun at their pointed helmets:

> It's really only the thought of storms
> that I find a little fright'ning –
> that spike on your Romantic heads
> might attract some modern lightning.
>
> *Deutschland: A Winter's Tale* 3.57-60, trans. T.J. Reed

Heine's status as an exile must have also stirred public interest in the poem, at least in some quarters, for his earlier work had already been banned in Germany, even before the publication of *Deutschland: A Winter's Tale*. After Napoleon's final defeat in 1815 and the end of his occupation of Germany, the Austrian Chancellor, Prince Klemens Metternich (1773-1859), had put his reactionary and conservative stamp on the Germanic Confederation and reinstated thirty-six German princes on their thrones, which fostered a closed and repressive political and intellectual climate in Germany (despite the burgeoning democratic sentiment in evidence at the time in other European countries). Typical of Metternich's policies were the Carlsbad decrees (1819), which set in place the policing of universities in order to monitor the activities of professors and students and thereby check the spread of radical ideas. This was not an ethos in which liberal thinkers and creative spirits could flourish, so in 1831 Heine took himself off to the more enlightened atmosphere of Paris, where he lived in exile, only returning home for a visit in the winter of 1843. It was this trip which inspired him to write his satire, documenting the exile's return to his beloved homeland, like some latterday Odysseus, and calling for radical change in the government and ethos of Germany. Heine is concerned throughout the satire with German national identity, both as it is and as it could be, and this is articulated powerfully in the stanzas about Arminius:

> This is the forest of Teutoburg,
> you probably know it from Tacitus.
> This is where Varus got himself stuck,
> the classic boggy morass it was.
>
> The Cheruscan prince defeated him here,
> Arminius, alias Hermann;
> the German principle won the day,
> the muck was also German.
>
> Just think, if Arminius' blonde horde
> had lost to the foreign foeman,
> would German liberty be what it is?
> We should have all been Roman.
>
> Rome's language and Rome's ways would reign,
> there'd be vestal virgins in Munich,
> those dear little Swabians would look so sweet
> in Roman toga or tunic.
>
> We'd have Hengstenberg as a haruspex,
> over ox's offal pondering,
> and Neander as augur on the watch
> for flocks of wild birds wandering.

Birch-Pfeiffer'd be swigging turpentine,
like Rome's ladies aristocratic.
(It's said that a side effect was to make
their urine aromatic.)
     Deutschland: A Winter's March 11.1-24, trans. T.J. Reed

Heine takes Arminius' slaughter of Varus and his legions, by
now the classic expression of German national pride, and
subversively imagines what would have happened if the
Germans had not won. Yet even the initial description of
Arminius' victory undermines the traditional patriotic overtones
of the episode, since Varus is well and truly stuck in the German
mud (which colludes with the Cheruscan price) and thus forms
an easy target for the German warriors. This is hardly the sort of
military victory to stir national pride, but instead seems
distinctly grubby, like the boggy locale in which the massacre
takes place. Moreover, the patriotism is further qualified when
Arminius himself is dubbed tribally as a 'Cheruscan prince',
rather than nationally as a German hero.

From that starting-point, the elaborate 'what if' sequence
which follows fantasises wryly about German identity as
'Romans'. The question is based on the deliberately erroneous
assumption that the very survival of Germany was at stake in
Arminius' confrontation with Varus. Indeed, the specific
mention of Tacitus is perhaps intended to point up the contra-
diction between the original Classical text and the later glories
of the idealised 'Arminius myth'. Moreover, Heine's question
about the fate of the cherished concept of German liberty in the
light of a Roman victory in AD 9 is highly acerbic in the context
of the poem so far: Arminius and his Cherusci did defeat Varus,

but the contemporary Germans appear to have tarnished their ancestors' legacy of liberty very effectively by themselves, despite the historical defeat of the oppressive Romans. Finally, the sequence of individual Germans engaging in stereotypical, but incongruous Roman activities is droll (and continues beyond the passage quoted). Thus, Ernst Wilhelm Hengstenberg (1802-69) and Wilhelm Neander (1789-1850) were Professors of Theology in Berlin, so they are aptly recast as a Roman sooth-sayer (*Haruspex*) and a diviner (*Augur*), both inappropriately pagan activities for these grand theologians. Charlotte Birch-Pfeiffer (1800-68) was a tragic actress and author of light plays, so she is remodelled as a languid Roman aristocratic lady, drinking turpentine, a popular Roman remedy for liver and kidney complaints (Pliny *Natural History* 23.144) or stomach upsets (Pliny *Natural History* 24.27). Perhaps Birch-Pfeiffer's pained facial expressions on the tragic stage mischievously prompted Heine to give her persistent ailments in his satire.

After concluding the 'what if' fantasy and expressing ironic thanks that Germans remained German, Heine ends the section by returning to Arminius:

> O Hermann, for all this we've you to thank!
> So at Detmold, as is fitting,
> they're building you a monument –
> I've even put my bit in.
> > *Deutschland: A Winter's March* 11.61-4, trans. T.J. Reed

Heine is referring here to what was to become perhaps the most conspicuous German celebration of Arminius, namely the famous statue of the national hero, erected near Detmold in the

Teutoberg forest. Whether Heine really made a financial contribution to the project is anybody's guess, but it seems unlikely. At any rate, the project at Detmold was started in 1838, and the statue was finally dedicated in 1875, after the establishment of the German empire in 1871, which was masterminded by the Prussian chancellor Otto von Bismarck (1815-98) and controlled by the Prussian emperor Wilhelm I (1797-1888). It was the sculptor Ernst von Bandel (1800-76) who conceived the project, in which he believed passionately, but its ambitious nature led to all sorts of financial difficulties (only resolved by Prussian intervention). Ernst von Bandel finally saw his visionary sculpture realised only one year before his death. The monumental statue and base together stand at about 53 metres high, an extraordinary sight (which visitors still flock to see). Arminius is wearing an archetypal winged helmet and holds his sword in his right hand raised proudly aloft. On the two sides of that sword are inscriptions: *German unity is my strength* and *My strength is Germany's might.* The words suggest an idealised and fruitfully symbiotic relationship between citizen and state.

The statue, whose prolonged genesis testifies to Germanic determination, held appeal not just for those living in Germany itself, but for those of German nationality living thousands of miles away. So in New Ulm, Minnesota, one of the city's founders, Julius Berndt (1832-1916), who had been born in Silesia, but came to America in 1852, decided in 1881 to build his own Hermann monument to adorn the town which he had helped to create. Work began in 1887, but the project (like its counterpart at Detmold) faced financial difficulties and was only completed in 1897. At the unveiling of the statue (about 31 metres tall, together with the base), about 20,000 people attended, brought in by special trains for the occasion. That Ernst von Bandel's original statue could be emulated so soon in another country is telling about its symbolic hold over people's imaginations.

The nineteenth century probably saw the zenith of Arminius' fame, but more recently there has been renewed interest in the man's legacy for different and exciting reasons. In 1987, a retired British officer, Major Tony Clunn, who has written an interesting book about his experiences, was exploring some fields near Kalkriese with a metal-detector, when he came across some hoards of Roman coins, all dated before AD 9. This discovery prompted him to speculate that the money had been buried for a reason and that he was close to the site of Arminius' ambush in the forest. When the archaeologists began to dig in earnest, weapons, tools and even a spectacular cavalry-officer's mask

Figure 7. Cavalry mask. Kalkriese Museum, Germany.

(Figure 7) came to light, as well as bones in a mass grave. It was fifty miles from the site of the jingoistic Hermann monument, but here at last was tangible archaeological evidence of the massacre of Varus' legions. In 2002, a museum was opened at Kalkriese to present the finds from the site (including the cavalry mask) to the general public. Finally, in the twenty-first century, it seems that the story of Arminius has run full circle. After all of these creative twists and turns in literature, drama and art over the centuries, we are reminded that the versatile myth has its roots in a real and bloody event, testified by the compelling discoveries made at Kalkriese.

Envoi

Tacitus remains a hugely compelling writer, whose naturally acerbic voice and brilliant creative talents (often more evocative of poetry than prose) were sharpened and intensified by the troubled era in which he lived. Without the evolving pressures imposed on the Roman aristocracy by the principate, Tacitus as a Classical author might never even have existed. Like George Orwell all those centuries later, he needed (and indeed thrived on) the peculiar and challenging circumstances of his own time as an impetus for writing.

Yet although his subject matter is drawn from his contemporary world, the phenomena which drove his creative processes – moral decline, hunger for power, hypocrisy, sycophancy, military might, the corruption of language for political purposes, death in high places – are unfortunately timeless and will always be relevant. That is partly, but not only, why people still read his works today. As a commentator on political corruption, Tacitus is unparalleled, and to engage with his uncompromising narratives is simultaneously a painful but mesmerising experience, further enhanced aesthetically by the fruitful marriage between his stylised Latin and his robust ideological stance. It is particularly striking that the most purple of all his purple passages – such as the visit of the Roman legions to the site of Varus' disaster (*Annals* 1.61-2) or the burning of the Capitoline temple during the civil war (*Histories* 3.71-2) – coincide with the most intense moments of collective shame for the Roman state.

Today, with cameras and recording mechanisms everywhere, our own cataclysms, whether tsunamis or terrorist attacks, are often recorded in real time, for immediate consumption on television, and we do not necessarily have a strong but reflective mediating voice to come between us and the unfolding events. When such media are not available, however, modern society still resorts to devices such as the docudrama to allow us to 'view' important events as they might have happened (such as the circumstances leading up to the suicide of the scientist and government adviser Dr David Kelly in 2003). Yet to see things in this manner, or even to witness them in person, is not necessarily to understand what has happened, however vivid the process of watching may feel at the time. This is where Tacitus is different, for although he zooms in on crucial scenes, presented with a vibrancy and attention to detail which makes a reader feel present in history, he also embeds such moments in a continuous critical narrative, which allows us to gain a sense of cause and effect and to analyse what it is that we are seeing. His measured authorial presence in selecting and presenting his material thus opens up for his readers a bigger picture and makes it possible to understand the past, however distressing that may sometimes be.

At the same time, Tacitus' motivation for writing is firmly rooted in the present (and also the future), as he uses the past to have an impact on the prevailing circumstances of his own day. History in his hands is a powerful weapon dexterously wielded by an expert to confront contemporary problems. It is true that men like Domitian and Agricola are dead and buried, but in preserving them for posterity so memorably, Tacitus poses perennial questions. What is the point at which personal integrity should take precedence over loyalty to the state? Does excessive power change people, or merely exacerbate pre-existing characteristics? How problematic is it to impose one's own political and imperial systems on other countries? Tacitus deals in particulars, rooted in a specific historical period, but the continuing relevance of his voice will be clear to anyone who now puts this book aside and goes off to read his works. I hope that I have conveyed at least some of the richness and complexity that makes Tacitus such a consummate intellect and a unique voice from the ancient world.

Further Reading

Translations

There are various translations of Tacitus' works available, although inevitably they vary in quality and accuracy. There is a Penguin edition of the *Agricola* and *Germania* (London 1973), translated by H. Mattingly and revised by S. Handford, but the Oxford World's Classics volume (Oxford 1999) translated by A. Birley is more up-to-date. J.B. Rives has also translated the *Germania* (Oxford 1999) in an excellent volume, which also has an extremely helpful introduction and commentary. The *Dialogus* is badly served for English translations, which means that readers are best advised to consult the Loeb edition, *Dialogus, Agricola, Germania* (Cambridge Mass. 1914, revised edition 1969), originally translated by W. Peterson and revised by M. Winterbottom. All of Tacitus' works are available in the Loeb series, which offers an English translation facing the Latin.

The major historical works are better served by a range of affordable modern translations. W.H. Fyfe's translation of the *Histories* in the World's Classics series (Oxford 1997), revised and edited by D.S. Levene, is accessible and accurate, while the Penguin translation by K. Wellesley (London 1995) is more distinctive and ornate (and is in the process of being revised), but both can be recommended. A.J. Woodman's translation of the *Annals* (Indianapolis and Cambridge 2004) strives to reproduce the flavour of Tacitus' distinctive Latin style in the English and is far preferable to M. Grant's Penguin (originally published in 1956, but reprinted with a new bibliography in 1989).

General books on Tacitus and Roman historiography

What follows is a selection from the many studies of Tacitus currently available, but it has been assembled with accessibility in mind and so I have restricted the references to books and volumes of essays. Although there is a rich collection of specialised articles on Tacitus to be found in academic journals, not all readers will have access to these (many of which are conveniently listed in the bibliographies of the works below), so it seems best to direct readers towards more readily available book-length studies.

The best place to start is with a pair of books, R. Martin, *Tacitus* (London 1981, revised 1994) and R. Mellor, *Tacitus* (London and New York 1993). These both offer clear and helpful introductions to the author and his works. Also to be recommended is C.S. Kraus and A.J. Woodman, *Latin Historians* (Oxford 1997). This collaborative project has a broader remit than Tacitus' works alone, but incisively brings to life the main protagonists of the genre and clarifies the complex relationship between them. In a similar spirit, readers will enjoy A.J. Woodman, *Rhetoric in Classical Historiography* (London and Sydney 1988), an important book which heralded an expansion of scholarly interest in Roman historiography, and J. Marincola, *Authority and Tradition in Ancient Historiography* (Cambridge 1997), an excellent and wide-ranging study, which also incorporates the Greek tradition and is now available in paperback. T.J. Luce and A.J. Woodman, *Tacitus and the Tacitean Tradition* (Princeton 1993), offer an edited volume with a broad focus, ranging from detailed studies of Tacitus' individual works to their later reception. More recently, A.J. Woodman has assembled and revised his most important articles on Tacitus in *Tacitus Reviewed* (Oxford 1998), a volume which will be particularly engaging for those with interests in Tacitus' Latin. Finally, a classic in the field is R. Syme, *Tacitus* (Oxford 1958), a rich and comprehensive study in two volumes by an unparalleled expert, whose pithy style often mirrors Tacitus' own.

If you want to focus on particular works of Tacitus, there are various possibilities. For the *Histories*, you can consult my own book, *Ordering Anarchy: Armies and Leaders in Tacitus' Histories* (London 1999), which is intended to be an intelligible study of Tacitus' elegant historiographical techniques in a work which long played second fiddle to the *Annals*. A very different analysis is H. Haynes, *The History of Make-Believe: Tacitus on Imperial Rome* (Berkeley, Los Angeles, London 2003), which approaches the text from an elaborate theoretical standpoint that new readers of Tacitus may find tricky, although those with specialised interests in literary theory will enjoy it. A similar contrast can be seen in two studies of the *Annals*: B. Walker, *The Annals of Tacitus* (Manchester 1952) is an excellent introduction to the text and is still well worth reading today, while E. O'Gorman, *Irony and Misreading in the Annals of Tacitus* (Cambridge 2000) is a study informed by literary theory, which those with specialised interests will appreciate, but it may be rather challenging for general readers as a first port of call. J. Ginsburg, *Tradition and Theme in the Annals of Tacitus* (New

York 1981), analyses Tacitus' subtle manipulation of the traditional annalistic framework particularly in *Annals* 1-6 and argues that thematic considerations often led him to allow considerable temporal dislocations of the historical material.

Works cited and additional material

I refer here to items specifically mentioned in discussion in this book, but I also include (marked with an asterisk) some particularly useful pieces not directly cited in the text:

*H.W. Benario, 'Tacitus' *Germania* and Modern Germany', *Illinois Classical Studies* 15 (1990) 163-75.

*H.W. Benario, 'Arminius into Hermann: History into Legend', *Greece and Rome* 51 (2004) 83-94.

T. Clunn, *In Quest of the Lost Legions* (second edition 2005).

R. Kühnemund, *Arminius, or the Rise of a National Symbol in Literature* (Chapel Hill NC 1953).

R. Martin, 'Tacitus and the Death of Augustus', *Classical Quarterly* 5 (1955) 123-8.

R. Mayer, 'Pliny and *Gloria Dicendi*', *Arethusa* 36 (2003) 227-34.

A. Pomeroy, 'Center and Periphery in Tacitus's *Histories*', *Arethusa* 36 (2003) 361-74.

I. Schöffer, 'The Batavian Myth during the Sixteenth and Seventeenth Centuries', 78-101 in J.S. Bromley and E.H. Kossmann (eds), *Britain and the Netherlands*, vol. V (The Hague 1975).

*K. Tilmans, 'Aeneas, Bato and Civilis, the Forefathers of the Dutch: the Origin of the Batavian Tradition in Dutch

Humanistic Historiography', 121-35 in J.R. Brink and W.F. Gentrup, *Renaissance Culture in Context: Theory and Practice* (Aldershot 1993).

*P. Wells, *The Battle that Stopped Rome: Emperor Augustus, Arminius and the Slaughter of the Legions in the Teutoburg Forest* (New York and London 2003).

Index